PIANO/VOCAL

THE
Wright & Forrest
SONGBOOK

Music, Lyrics and Adaptations by
Robert Wright & George Forrest

ISBN 0-634-06525-4

Scheffel Music Corp.

7777 W. BLUEMOUND RD. P.O. BOX 13819 MILWAUKEE, WI 53213

Visit Hal Leonard Online at
www.halleonard.com

THE
Wright & Forrest
SONGBOOK

Wright & Forrest

Robert Craig (Bob) Wright, born Daytona Beach, Florida, September 25, 1914.

George (Chet) Chichester, Jr. (George Forrest), born Brooklyn, New York, July 31, 1915, died October 10, 1999.

Bob Wright remembers:

We met as sophomores in Miami Senior High when Chet vocally auditioned for Professor O.F. Steinmetz. Already a professional musician, I was the accompanist for the Glee Club. Chet, blessed with perfect pitch and an acute ear, waived any accompaniment and flawlessly sang at sight every syllable and note of the rousing choral piece "Rolling Down to Rio." Professor Steinmetz, clearly impressed, welcomed Chet, cautioning his other tenors: "Sing what Mr. Chichester sings. Don't ask me! If *he* makes a mistake—there's a *misprint* in the music!"

I was intrigued by Chet's triumph and easy, casual musicianship. For me, Chet's talent was of a new and rare order. While I was talented, Chet was touched with genius.

Next day, making the climb to the fourth floor music room, a well-played cascade of current Broadway show tunes echoed down the stairwell—with the correct chords. Of course, it was Chet. Show tunes—with the right harmonies? We became friendlier.

Weeks later, Professor Steinmetz, seeing us together, said he heard we both, separately, wrote pop songs. Would we, together, write a fight song for the cheerleaders? The result was our first collaboration:

> HAIL TO MIAMI HIGH!
> FOR YOU WE DO OR DIE!
> STARTING GUN TO FINISH BELL
> FOR YOU WE WILL YELL LIKE HELL!
> YELL FOR MY MIAMI,
> FOR MY MIAMI HIGH!
> (yells)
> FIGHT! FIGHT! FIGHT!

This was the first of more than seventy years of music and hundreds of lyrics and melodies for screen, stage, recordings and television. More than fifty filing cabinets full of our scores and special material stand in our music studios in Miami and New York. But back then, hearing our music *sung* for the first time opened new vistas. This is what we both wanted: to create music together and hear it performed.

And we did it. In the movies, our first big film was *Maytime*, and we went on to write songs and musical sequences for many, many other pictures at MGM and other studios. Following the attack on Pearl Harbor we moved to New York City. For four or five years we lived at the Algonquin Hotel, where we wrote, directed and produced shows and cabaret acts for clubs like the Copacabana. In lieu of being drafted, we were hired by the Treasury Department to create patriotic songs and special material to boost morale and productivity during the war years.

In 1944 our professional relationship with Edwin Lester was solidified when he produced our first musical, *Song of Norway*. From then on we wrote something for him nearly every year for twenty years. He taught us everything about all aspects of musicals and the theater business. Yet he was more than a collaborative guide; as our producer, he presented many of our biggest hits.

When we began writing *Kismet*, we played a few of the songs for Frank Loesser, who immediately decided to direct our careers, and we were with him until his death. In addition to making us a fortune from our songs, Frank was a true champion of us and our music. He was a friend, an inspiration and a mentor.

We wrote many shows during the following years, but it would take more than thiry-five years for *Grand Hotel* to make it to Broadway. Our collaborator, Luther Davis, wrote the first version in the mid-1950s. *At the Grand* was first presented by Edwin Lester for his Los Angeles and San Francisco Light Opera Companies. Although it was enormously successful, the production closed prematurely due to the illness of our star, Paul Muni.

But in the late 1980s, the conductor Jack Lee heard our score and brought the show to Tommy Tune's attention. We had seen Tommy's direction of the Off-Broadway play *Cloud Nine*, and we suggested that he ought to be the director for the Broadway production of *Grand Hotel, The Musical*. Finally our show would be presented successfully.

Though it was not planned, by us anyway, we have lived in the great cities of commercial music: Hollywood, New York, London and Miami. And we've been blessed with great successes as we achieved our ambitions.

Thank you to Hal Leonard Corporation for publishing this collection of our songs, and their enthusiastic support and artistic and editorial guidance.

Enjoy!

Robert Wright

Wright & Forrest

MEMBERS:

American Society of Composers, Authors and Publishers (1939 to present)
The Songwriters' Guild (formerly, the American Guild of Authors and Composers)
The Dramatists Guild
The Players

AWARDS AND HONORS:

Three Academy Award nominations for Best Song:
1938   "Always and Always" from *Mannequin* (MGM)
1940   "It's a Blue World" from *Music in My Heart* (Columbia)
1942   "Pennies for Pepino" from *Fiesta* (Hal Roach)
1953-1954 Antoinette Perry Award, Outstanding Musical Score, for *Kismet*
1990   Two Drama Desk nominations for music and lyrics, and nominations for
                Antoinette Perry Award, Best Original Music Score, for *Grand Hotel: The Musical*
1995   Richard Rodgers/ASCAP Award for Outstanding Lifetime Contributions to the
                American Musical Theatre

THEATRICAL CREDITS

As lyricists and composers (or adaptors) (with places of first performances):
- THANK YOU, COLUMBUS – Hollywood Playhouse, Los Angeles (1940)
- SONG OF NORWAY – Philharmonic Auditorium, Los Angeles (1944)
- SPRING IN BRAZIL – Shubert Theatre, Boston (1945-1946)
- GYPSY LADY – Philharmonic Auditorium, Los Angeles (1947, also directors)
- MAGDALENA – Philharmonic Auditorium, Los Angeles (1948)
- THE GREAT WALTZ – Philharmonic Auditorium, Los Angeles (1949 and 1953)
- KISMET – Philharmonic Auditorium, Los Angeles (1953-1955); Ziegeld Theatre, New York (1953)
- THE CAREFREE HEART (also book authors) – Cass Theatre, Detroit (1957)
- AT THE GRAND – Philharmonic Auditorium, Los Angeles; Curran Theatre, San Francisco (1958)
- KEAN – Shubert Theatre, Boston (1961)
- ANYA – Ziegfeld Theatre, New York (1965)
- DUMAS AND SON – Dorothy Chandler Pavillion, Los Angeles (1967)
- A SONG FOR CYRANO (A new translation of Edmond Rostand's *Cyrano de Bergerac*, by and starring José Ferrer) – National Summer Tour (1973)
- TIMBUKTU! (the African *Kismet*) – Shubert Theatre, Philadelphia (1978); Mark Hellinger Theatre, New York (1978)
- GRAND HOTEL: THE MUSICAL – Colonial Theatre, Boston (1989); Gershwin Theatre, New York (1989)
- ANASTASIA: THE MUSICAL (A play with music based on themes of Sergei Rachmaninoff) – premiere performance at Lowell Repertory Theatre, Lowell, Massachusetts (November, 1989)

As lyricists, composers and adaptors of revised versions of additional stage musicals:
- NAUGHTY MARIETTA – Philharmonic Auditorium (1940)
- RIO RITA – Philharmonic Auditorium, Los Angeles; Curran Theatre, San Francisco (1941)
- THE FIREFLY (for Allan Jones) – Hollywood Bowl, Los Angeles (1941)
- FUN FOR THE MONEY – Hollywood Playhouse, Los Angeles (1941)
- ZIEGFELD FOLLIES – Shubert Theatre, Boston; Winter Garden Theatre, New York (1942)

- CLIFFORD FISCHER'S FOLIES BERGERE – Edison Theatre, Edison Hotel, New York (1943)
- LOU WALTERS' ARTISTS AND MODELS – Opera House, Boston; Century Theatre, New York (1946)
- RED, WHITE AND BLUE – Paramount Downtown Theatre, Los Angeles (1950)

As directors, producers, lyricists and composers of numerous original songs:
- Eleven Camp Tamiment Theater Revues – Tamiment Playhouse, Stroudsburg, Pennsylvania (1942)
- Six Copacabana Cabaret Revues, New York (1942-1943)
- Vaughan Monroe's Commodore Hotel Revue – Commodore Hotel, New York (1943)
- Three Colonial Inn Casino Revues – Hollywood, Florida (1945-1948)

As creators of nightclub acts and special material for:
The Barry Sisters (1943), Helena Bliss (1951), Ray Bourbon (1935), Lawrence Brooks (1942), Imogene Coca (1943), Gloria De Haven (1950), Jimmy Durante (1942), Kent Edwards (1946-1949), Jean Fenn (1945), Martha French (1942), Jane Froman (1942-1956), Celeste Holm (1943), Mary Howard (1945), Anne Jeffreys and Robert Sterling (1952-1953), Della Norell (1943), Nadya Norskaya (1946), Spivy (1942), Sophie Tucker (1940, MGM)

SCREEN CREDITS

As lyricists and composers/adaptors of songs)

NEW SHOES (short) (Metro-Goldwyn-Mayer, 1936)
Stars: Arthur Lake, Jean Chatburn, Jo Stafford Trio

THE LONGEST NIGHT (MGM, 1936)
Stars: Robert Young, Florence Rice, Julie Haydon

AFTER THE THIN MAN (MGM, 1936)
Stars: William Powell, Myrna Loy, Elissa Landi, James Stewart

LIBELED LADY (MGM, 1936)
Stars: William Powell, Myrna Loy, Spencer Tracy, Jean Harlow

SINNER TAKES ALL (MGM, 1936)
Stars: Margaret Lindsay, Bruce Cabot

MAYTIME (MGM, 1937)
Stars: John Barrymore, Jeanette MacDonald, Nelson Eddy

ROSALIE (MGM, 1937)
Stars: Nelson Eddy, Eleanor Powell, Ray Bolger, Edna May Oliver
Score: Cole Porter

THE GOOD OLD SOAK (MGM, 1937)
Stars: Wallace Beery, Una Merkel, Ted Healy, Betty Furness

LONDON BY NIGHT (MGM, 1937)
Stars: George Murphy, Virginia Field, Eddie Quillan

MADAME "X" (MGM, 1937)
Stars: Gladys George, John Beal, Warren William

MAMA STEPS OUT (MGM, 1937)
Stars: Alice Brady, Guy Kibbee, Betty Furness, Dennis Morgan

MANNEQUIN (MGM, 1937)
Stars: Joan Crawford, Spencer Tracy, Alan Curtis

MAN OF THE PEOPLE (MGM, 1937)
Stars: Joseph Calleia, Thomas Mitchell, Florence Rice

NAVY BLUE AND GOLD (MGM, 1937)
Stars: Lionel Barrymore, Robert Young, Tom Brown, James Stewart

PARNELL (MGM, 1937)
    Stars: Clark Gable, Myrna Loy, Edna May Oliver, Billie Burke
SARATOGA (MGM, 1937)
    Stars: Jean Harlow, Clark Gable, Walter Pidgeon, Lionel Barrymore
THE FIREFLY (MGM, 1937)
    Stars: Jeanette MacDonald, Allan Jones, Warren William
HITTING A NEW HIGH (RKO, 1937)
    Stars: Lily Pons, Edward Everett Horton
THE BADMAN OF BRIMSTONE (MGM, 1937)
    Stars: Wallace Beery, Dennis O'Keefe, Cliff Edwards, Bruce Cabot, Virginia Bruce,
    Lewis Stone, Noah Beery
YOU'RE ONLY YOUNG ONCE (MGM, 1938)
    Stars: Lewis Stone, Fay Holden, Mickey Rooney, Cecilia Parker
BOYS TOWN (MGM, 1938)
    Stars: Spencer Tracy, Mickey Rooney
THE FIRST HUNDRED YEARS (MGM, 1938)
    Stars: Robert Montgomery, Virginia Bruce, Lee Bowman, Binnie Barnes
LORD JEFF (MGM, 1938)
    Stars: Mickey Rooney, Freddie Bartholomew, Charles Coburn, Peter Lawford
MARIE ANTOINETTE (MGM, 1938)
    Stars: Norma Shearer, Tyrone Power, Robert Morley, Joseph Schildkraut, Anita Louise,
    John Barrymore, Gladys George, Henry Daniell, Joseph Calleia
SWEETHEARTS (MGM, 1938)
    Stars: Jeanette MacDonald, Nelson Eddy, Ray Bolger, Frank Morgan, Florence Rice,
    Gene and Kathleen Lockhart
THREE COMRADES (MGM, 1938)
    Stars: Margaret Sullavan, Robert Taylor, Franchot Tone, Robert Young
THE TOY WIFE (MGM, 1938)
    Stars: Luise Rainer, Robert Young, Melvyn Douglas, Barbara O'Neil, H.B. Warner,
    Alma Kruger
VACATION FROM LOVE (MGM, 1938)
    Stars: Dennis O'Keefe, June Knight, Edward Brophy, Florence Rice
HAPPILY BURIED (MGM, short feature, 1938)
    Producer: Jack Chertok
THE MAGICIAN'S DAUGHTER (MGM, 1938)
    Producer: Jack Chertok
NUTS AND BOLTS (MGM, 1938)
    Producer: Jack Chertok
OUR GANG FOLLIES (MGM, 1938)
    Producer: Hal Roach
SNOW GETS IN YOUR EYES (MGM, 1938)
    Producer: Jack Chertok
HONOLULU (MGM, 1938)
    Stars: Eleanor Powell, Robert Young, George Burns, Gracie Allen, Rita Johnson,
    Ruth Hussey
THE SHOPWORN ANGEL (MGM, 1938)
    Stars: Margaret Sullavan, James Stewart, Walter Pidgeon, Hattie McDaniel

THE GIRL DOWNSTAIRS (MGM, 1938)
Stars: Franciska Gaal, Franchot Tone, Rita Johnson, Walter Connolly

THE HARDYS RIDE HIGH (MGM, 1939)
Stars: Lewis Stone, Mickey Rooney

LET FREEDOM RING (MGM, 1938)
Stars: Nelson Eddy, Edward Arnold, Victor McLaglen, Lionel Barrymore,
Virginia Bruce, Guy Kibbee, H.B. Warner

BROADWAY SERENADE (MGM, 1938)
Stars: Jeanette MacDonald, Lew Ayres, Ian Hunter

THE WOMEN (MGM, 1938)
Stars: Norma Shearer, Joan Crawford, Rosalind Russell, Joan Fontaine, Mary Boland,
Paulette Godard, Ruth Hussey, Marjorie Main, Hedda Hopper

BALALAIKA (MGM, 1938)
Stars: Nelson Eddy, Ilona Massey, Charles Ruggles, Frank Morgan, C. Aubrey Smith,
Lionel Atwill

THESE GLAMOUR GIRLS (MGM, 1939)
Stars: Lana Turner, Lew Ayres, Tom Brown, Owen Davis, Jr., Richard Carlson,
Peter Lind Hayes, Ann Rutherford, Jane Bryan, Anita Louise, Marsha Hunt

FLORIAN (MGM, 1940)
Stars: Florian, The Lipizzaner Stallion, Robert Young, Helen Gilbert, Charles Coburn
Lee Bowman, Reginald Owen, S.Z. Sakall, Irina Baronova

STRANGE CARGO (MGM, 1940)
Stars: Clark Gable, Joan Crawford, Peter Lorre, Paul Lukas

NEW MOON (MGM, 1940)
Stars: Jeanette MacDonald, Nelson Eddy, Mary Boland, H.B. Warner, George Zucco

MUSIC IN MY HEART (Columbia, 1940)
Stars: Tony Martin, Rita Hayworth, Douglas Dumbrille, Kay Thompson

DANCE, GIRL, DANCE (RKO, 1940)
Stars: Lucille Ball, Louis Hayward, Maureen O'Hara, Virginia Field, Ralph Bellamy,
Mary Carlisle, Katharine Alexander, Edward Brophy, Walter Abel, Harold Huber,
Maria Ouspenskaya

SOUTH OF PAGO-PAGO (United Artists, 1940)
Stars: Victor McLaglen, Jon Hall, Frances Farmer, Gene Lockhart, Douglas Dumbrille,
Olympe Bradna

KIT CARSON (United Artists, 1940)
Stars: Jon Hall, Lynn Bari, Dana Andrews, Ward Bond, Harold Huber

BLONDIE GOES LATIN (Columbia, 1941)
Stars: Penny Singleton, Arthur Lake

CUBANA (Hal Roach, 1941)

FIESTA (Hal Roach, 1941)
Stars: Anne Ayars, George Negrete, Armida, George Givot, Antonio Moreno

FLYING WITH MUSIC (Hal Roach, 1941)

RIO RITA (MGM, 1941)
Stars: Bud Abbott and Lou Costello, Kathryn Grayson, John Carroll, Barry Nelson,
Tom Conway

I MARRIED AN ANGEL (MGM, 1942)
Stars: Jeanette MacDonald, Nelson Eddy, Anne Jeffreys, Janis Carter, Marion Rosamond,
Mona Maris, Edward Everett Horton, Binnie Barnes, Reginald Owen, Douglas Dumbrille

RAINBOW 'ROUND MY SHOULDER (Columbia, 1942)
   Stars: Frankie Laine, Billy Daniels, Charlotte Austin, Arthur Franz

PICNIC (Columbia, 1955)
   Stars: William Holden, Kim Novak, Betty Field, Susan Strasberg, Cliff Robertson,
   and costarring Rosalind Russell as Rosemary

KISMET (MGM, 1955)
   Stars: Howard Keel, Anne Blythe, Dolores Gray, Vic Damone, Monte Wooley,
   Sebastian Cabot

SONG OF NORWAY (Cinerama, 1969)
   Stars: Florence Henderson, Toralv Maurstad, Frank Porretta, Christina Schollin,
   Oscar Homolka, Robert Morley, Edward G. Robinson, Harry Secombe

TAKING OFF (Universal, 1971)
   Stars: Lynn Carlin, Buck Henry, Georgia Engel, Audra Lindley, Paul Benedict

THE GREAT WALTZ (MGM, 1972)
   Stars: Horst Bucholz, Mary Costa, Rossano Brazzi

RADIO DAYS (Orion, 1987)
   Stars: Woody Allen, Julie Kavner, Danielle Ferland, Wallace Shawn

TELEVISION CREDITS

As lyricists and composers:

- "Star Time Hour" (Dumont, 1950-1951). Producers and directors, composers and lyricists of
  original music for 13 one-hour variety specials starring: Benny Goodman, Frances Langford,
  Lew Parker, Dick Haymes, Jack Cassidy, Lawrence Brooks, D'Argena, and others.
- "Stranger in Paradise" Tony Bennett television special (PBS, 1988)

RADIO CREDITS

As lyricists and composers and script writers:

- Maxwell House-MGM "Good News" (NBC, 1937-1938). Musical variety hour starring Fanny Brice,
  Judy Garland, Allan Jones, Meredith Willson, and others from the MGM "Stable of Stars"
- "Vicks Radio Hour" (NBC, 1939-1940). Weekly radio program starring Nelson Eddy.
- "Tune-Up Time" (NBC, 1940). Andre Kostelanetz, Kay Thompson, and others.
- "U.S. Treasury Star Parade" (1942-1943). Broadcast on all national networks, as well as Army Air
  Force and Marine stations in war theaters. Hosted by Janet Gaynor and Fredric March, with all-star
  casts changed weekly.
- The Woodbury Radio Hour (1945-1946). With Al Jolson.

RECORDINGS

As lyricists, composers/adaptors:

There are approximately 50 recorded albums of Wright and Forrest shows, and more than 2,000 single
recordings of Wright and Forrest songs. Additionally, dozens of films featuring scores and songs by
Wright and Forrest have been released on video and DVD.

THE
Wright & Forrest
SONGBOOK

Always And Always

from the MGM Motion Picture MANNEQUIN
(sung by Joan Crawford)

Lyrics by
BOB WRIGHT and CHET FORREST

Music by
ED WARD

Moderately, with expression

poco rall.

mf legato

Poco rubato

This world is full of love-ly things to see and do.

mp colla voce

But all its love-li-ness it brings to me through you,

You, love, are such a thrill, You make the world stand still! For

poco rall.

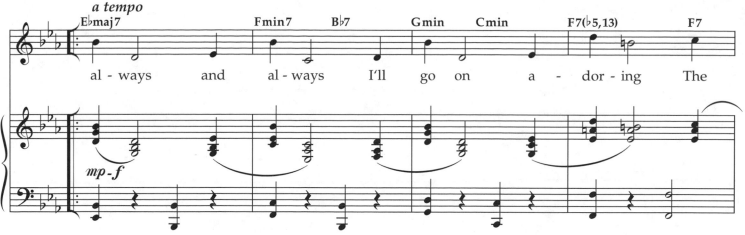

al - ways and al - ways I'll go on a - dor - ing The

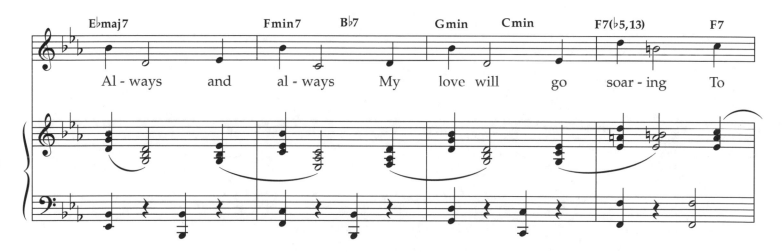

glo - ry and won - der of you!

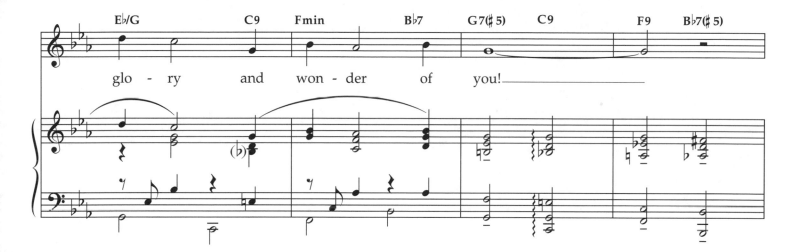

Al - ways and al - ways My love will go soar - ing To

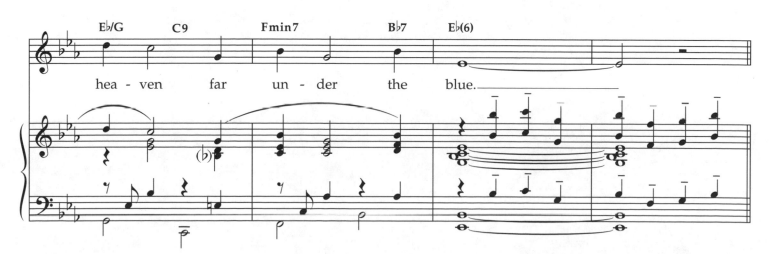

hea - ven far un - der the blue.

a tempo

Ebmaj7 / Fmin7 / Bb7

we'll be to - geth - er, For -

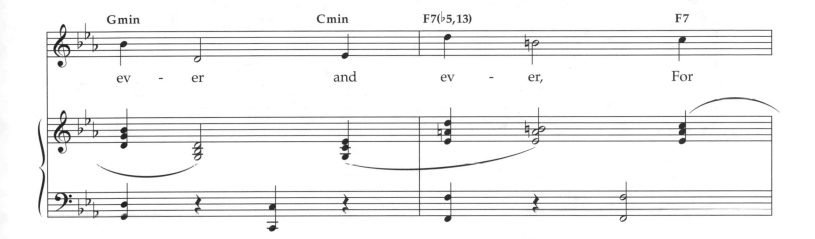

Gmin / Cmin / F7(b5,13) / F7

ev - er and ev - er, For

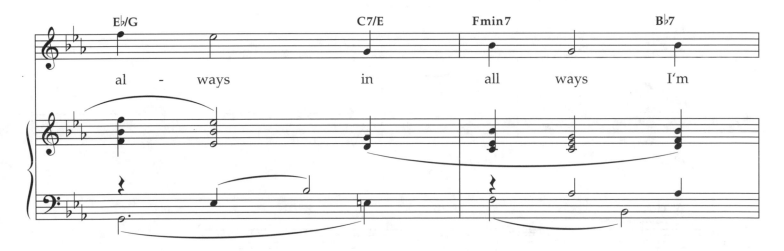

Eb/G / C7/E / Fmin7 / Bb7

al - ways in all ways I'm

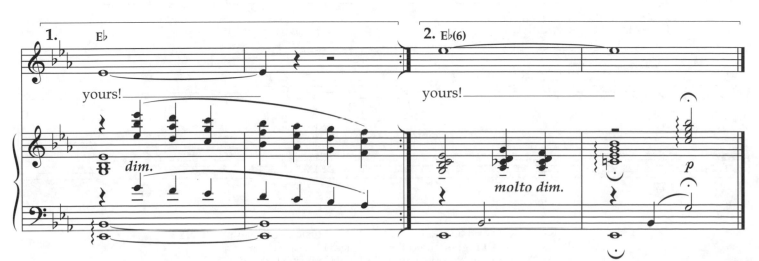

1. Eb

yours!

2. Eb(6)

yours!

dim.

molto dim.

p

And This Is My Beloved

from the MGM Motion Picture Musical **KISMET**
(sung by Ann Blyth)

Words and Music by
ROBERT WRIGHT and GEORGE FORREST
Music Based on Themes of A. Borodin

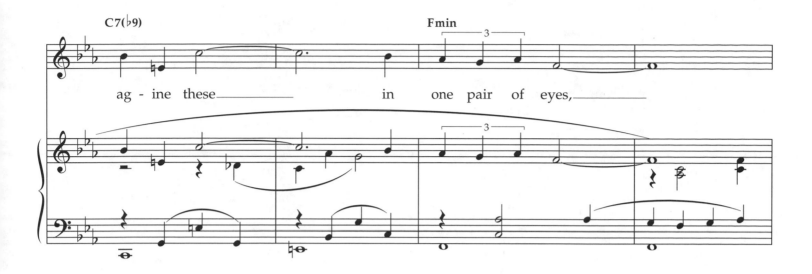

ag - ine these_____ in one pair of eyes,_____

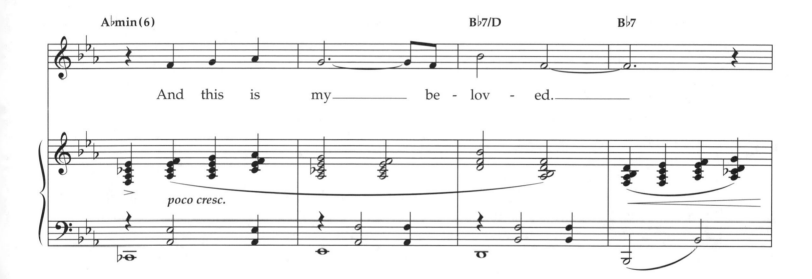

And this is my_____ be - lov - ed._____

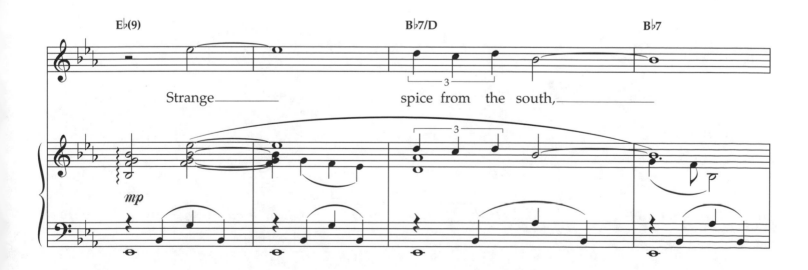

Strange_____ spice from the south,_____

Hon - ey through the comb_____ sift - ing;_____ Im -

ag - ine these_____ on one eag - er mouth,_____

And this is my_____ be - lov - ed._____

Con poco moto

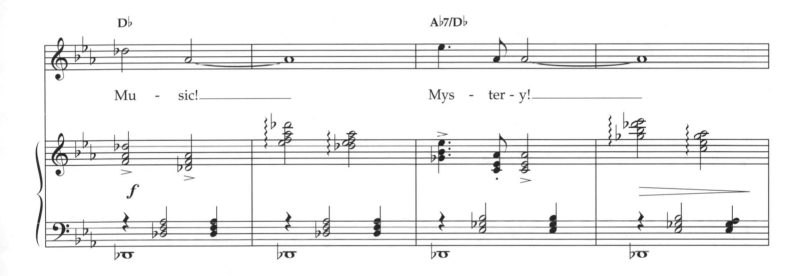

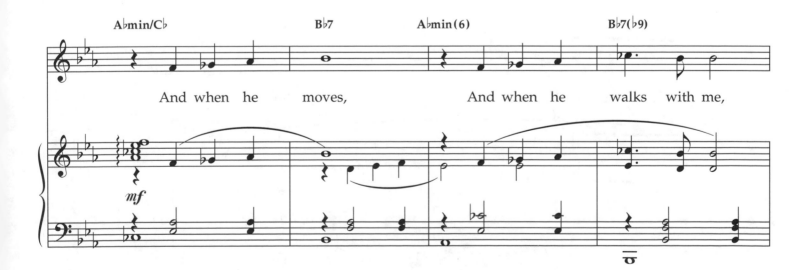

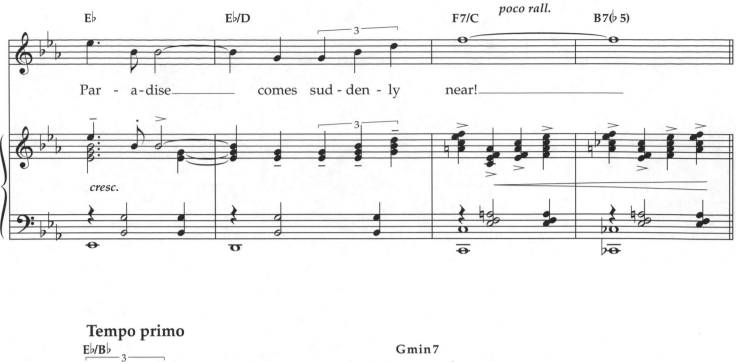

Par - a - dise comes sud - den - ly near!

Tempo primo

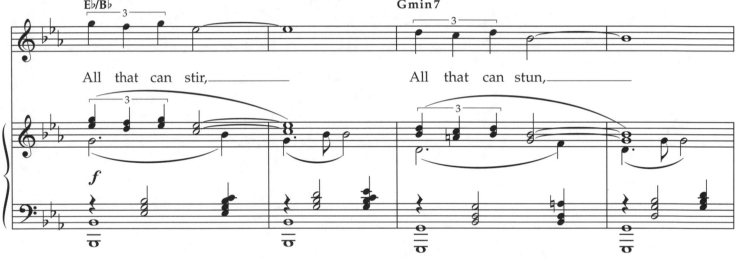

All that can stir, All that can stun,

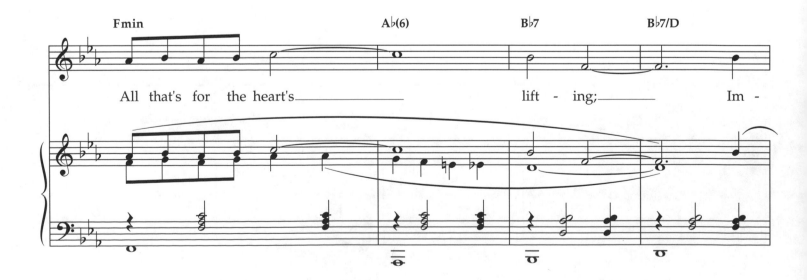

All that's for the heart's lift - ing; Im -

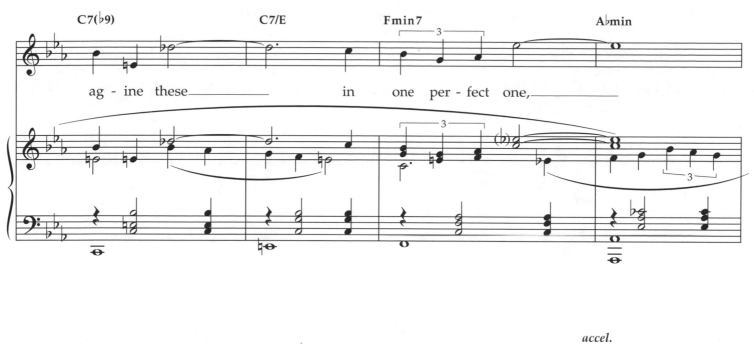

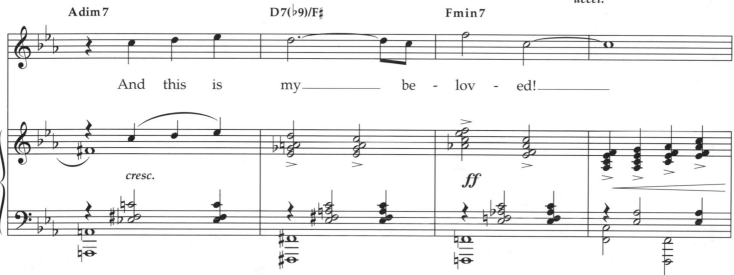

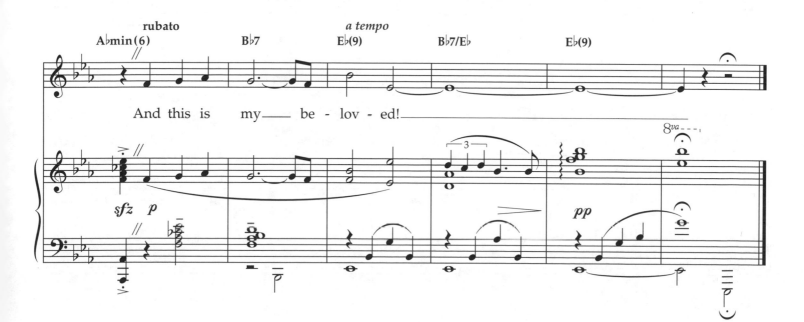

At The Balalaika

*from the MGM Motion Picture **BALALAIKA***
(sung by Nelson Eddy and Ilona Massey)

Lyrics by
ERIC MASCHWITZ
New Lyrics by
BOB WRIGHT and CHET FORREST

Music by
GEORGE PATSFORD
Music adapted by
HERBERT STOTHART

Moderately

a tempo

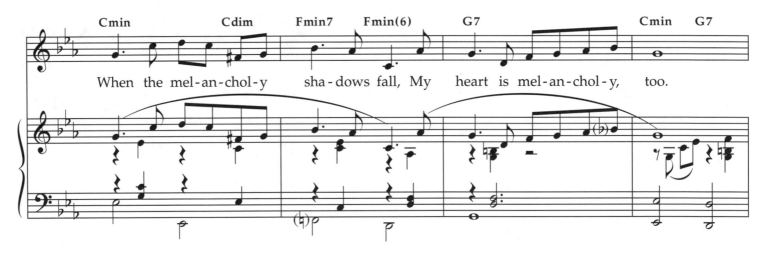

When the mel-an-chol-y sha-dows fall, My heart is mel-an-chol-y, too.

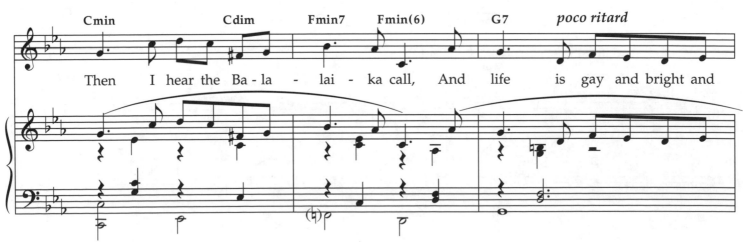

Then I hear the Ba-la - lai - ka call, And life is gay and bright and

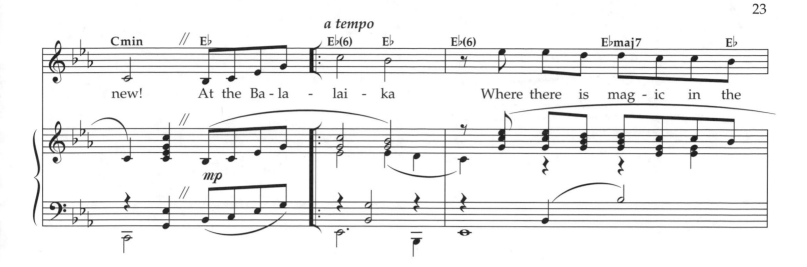

At the Ba - la - lai - ka Where there is mag - ic in the

spark - ling wine, And mel - low mus - ic in the can - dles shine

I have a ren - dez - vous! At the Ba - la -

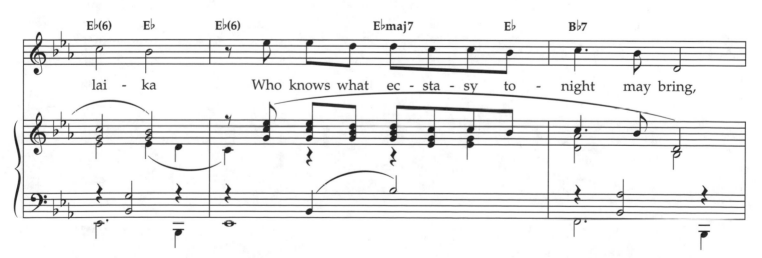

lai - ka Who knows what ec - sta - sy to - night may bring,

What love-ly mel-o-dy my heart may sing_____ Be-fore the night is

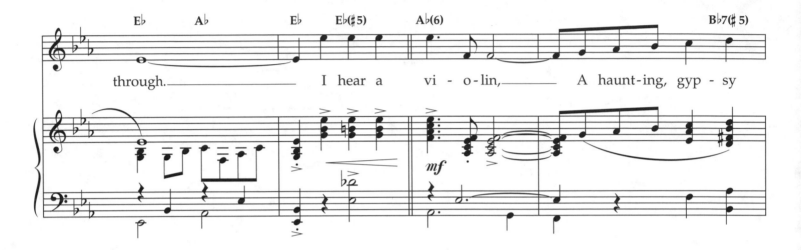

through._____ I hear a vi-o-lin,_____ A haunt-ing, gyp-sy

vi-o-lin._____ And when it sighs its strange-ly ten-der

song, I know that I be-long At the Ba-la-

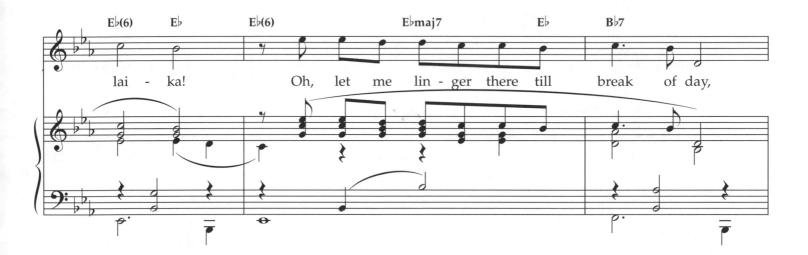

lai - ka! Oh, let me lin - ger there till break of day,

Where hearts are young and Ba - la - lai - kas play,_____ I have a ren - dez -

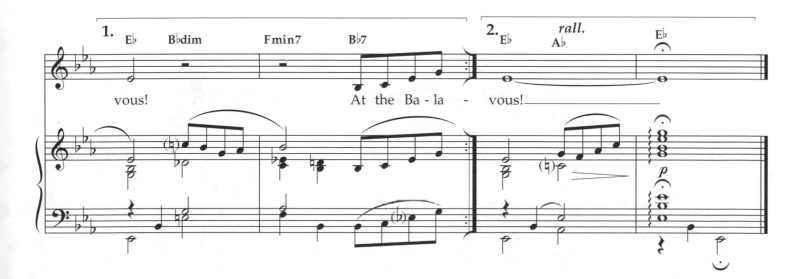

vous! At the Ba - la - vous!_____

Baubles, Bangles And Beads

from the Motion Picture Musical **KISMET**
(sung by Ann Blyth)

Words and Music by
ROBERT WRIGHT and GEORGE FORREST
Music Based on Themes of A. Borodin

Andante

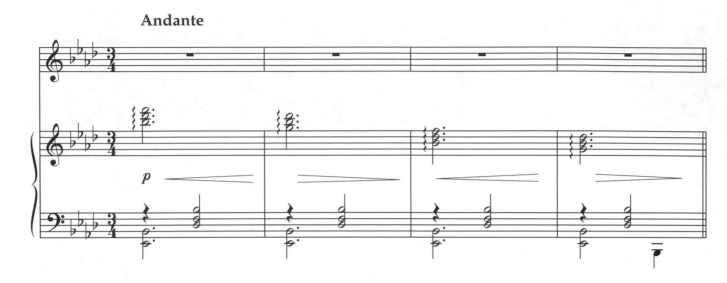

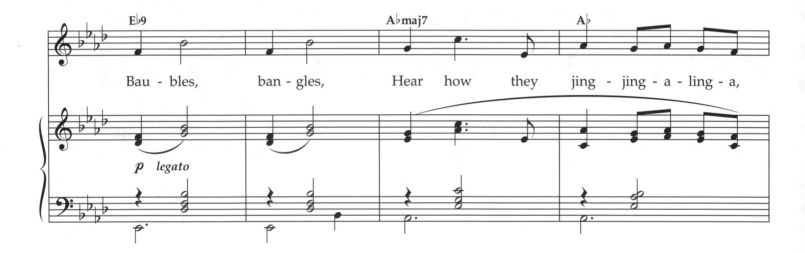

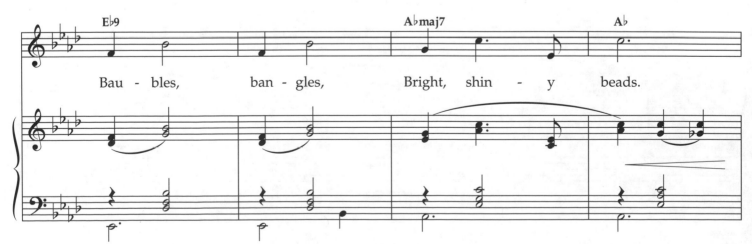

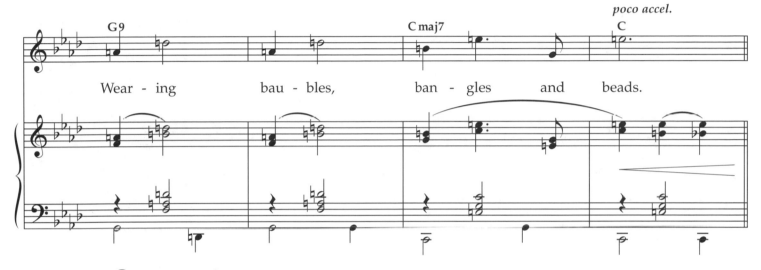

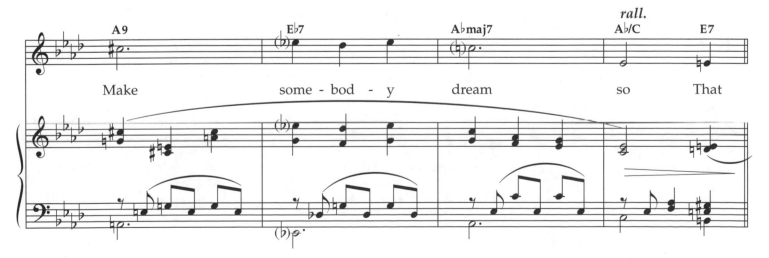

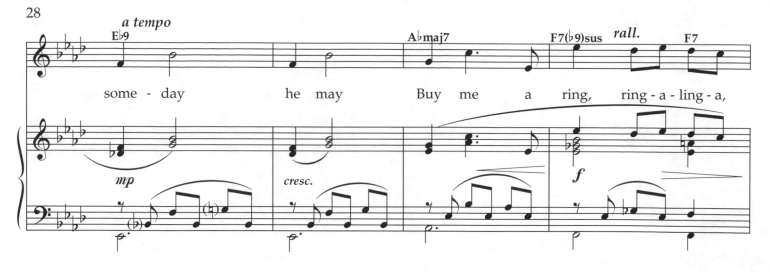

some - day   he may   Buy me   a   ring,   ring - a - ling - a,

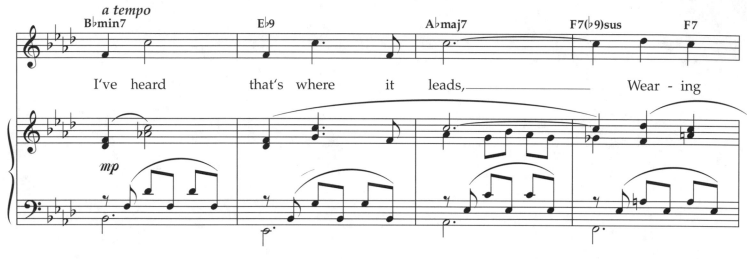

I've heard   that's where   it   leads,_____ Wear - ing

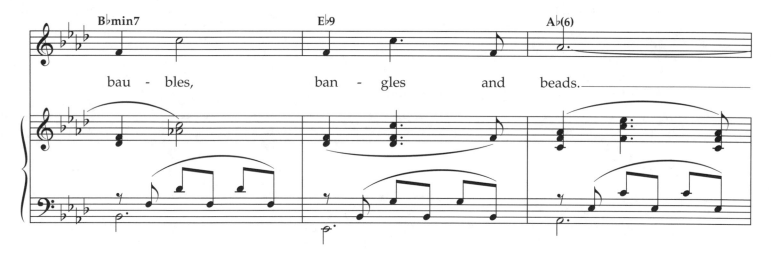

bau - bles,   ban - gles   and   beads._____

Freddy And His Fiddle

from the Musical SONG OF NORWAY
(sung by Janet Hamer and Kent Edwards)

Words and Music by
GEORGE CHET FORREST and ROBERT WRIGHT
based on themes of Edvard Grieg

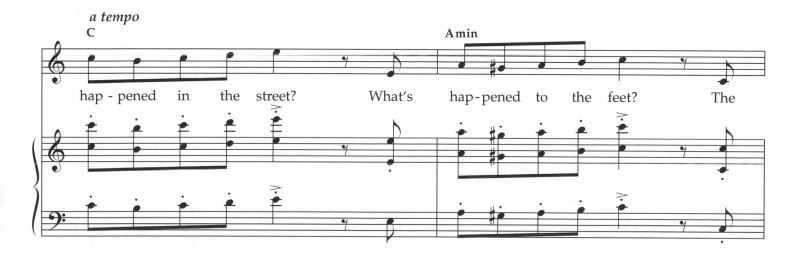

I can't dance, You can't dance, But let's ad-mit we're def-in-ite-ly dan-cing. That it's a phe-nom-en-on, no-bo-dy doubts; Yet it's ver-y com-mon on nights here a-bouts. Fred-dy and his fid-dle are

at it in the square a-gain and Fred-dy and his fid-dle make an-y-bo-dy dance! Make

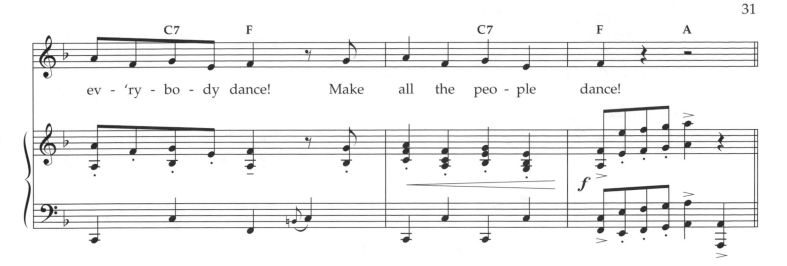

ev - 'ry - bo - dy dance! Make all the peo - ple dance!

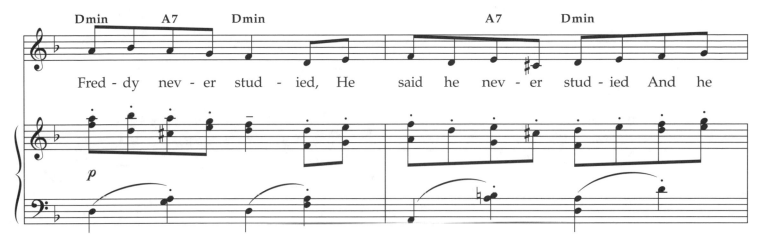

Fred - dy nev - er stud - ied, He said he nev - er stud - ied And he

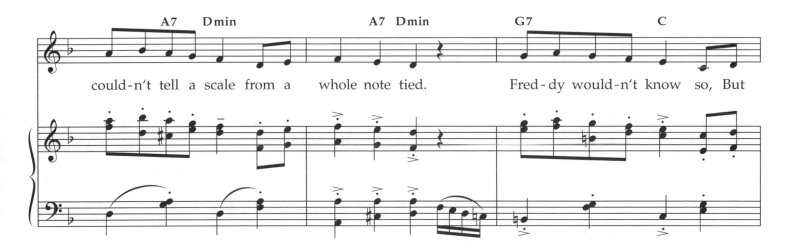

could-n't tell a scale from a whole note tied. Fred - dy would-n't know so, But

he's a vir - tu - o - so, When he pulls a horse-'s tail 'cross a cat's in - side! He'll

The Donkey Serenade

from the MGM Motion Picture Musical **THE FIREFLY**
(Sung by Allan Jones)

By
RUDOLF FRIML and HERBERT STOTHART

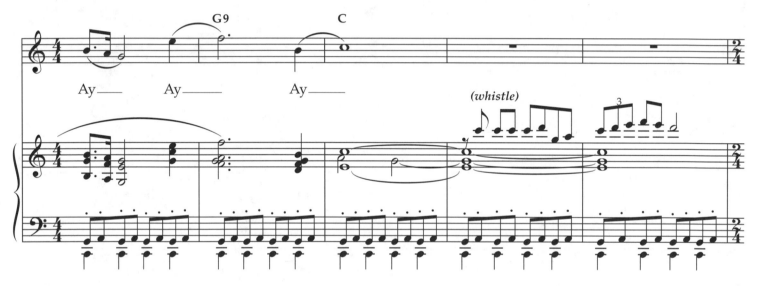

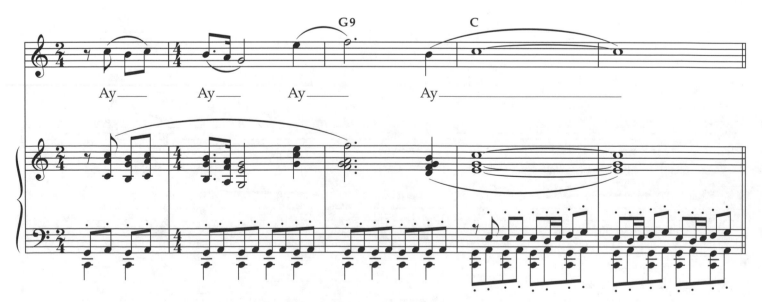

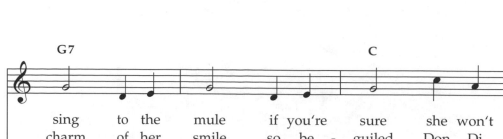

sing to the mule if you're sure she won't think that I am just a
charm of her smile so be - guiled Don Di - e - go that he rode a

fool ser - en - ad - ing a mule!
mile for the charm of her smile!

(to Boy with whistle)

A - mi - go mi - o, does she not have a dain - ty bray?
A - mi - go mi - o, is she lis - ten - ing to my song?

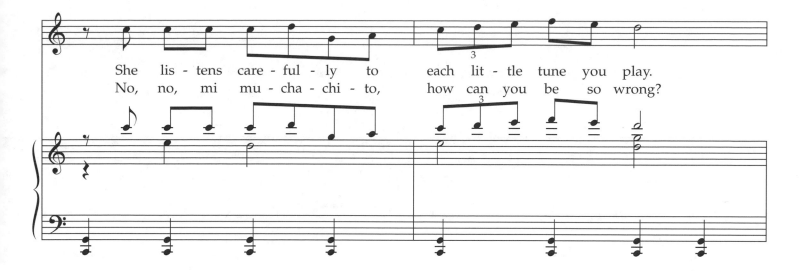

She lis - tens care - ful - ly to each lit - tle tune you play.
No, no, mi mu - cha - chi - to, how can you be so wrong?

Boy (spoken):
"La bella senorita?"

Si, si, mi mu - cha - chi - to,
Si, si, la se - nor - i - ta,

She'd love to sing it too, if on - ly she knew the way. But
(whistle) Her

E7

try as she may, in her voice there's a
face is a dream like an an - gel I

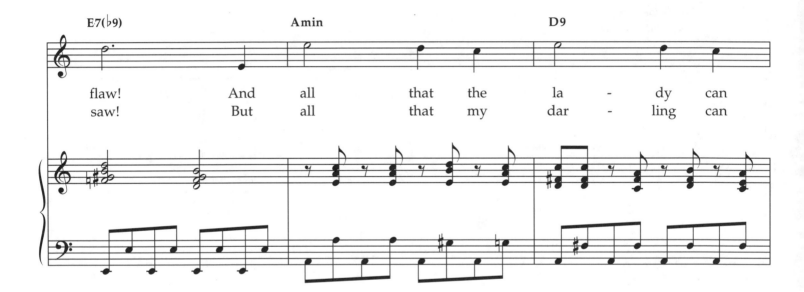

flaw! And all that the la - dy can
saw! But all that my dar - ling can

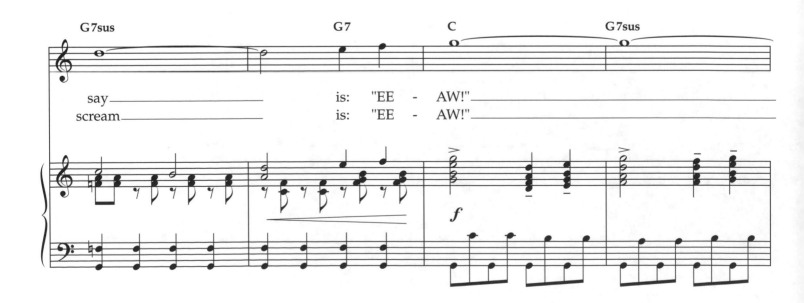

say_____ is: "EE - AW!"_____
scream_____ is: "EE - AW!"_____

The Grand Tango
(A Table with a View)
from the Musical GRAND HOTEL

Words and Music by
ROBERT WRIGHT and GEORGE FORREST

I want to sit

Where I can sit   And watch the world walk   by;

I want to go to the Grand Ca-fe,— Where life be-gins at the

end of day,— And let them show me to—

A lit - tle ta - ble with a view.

And as I sit, I'll sip a bit, And sigh a hap-py

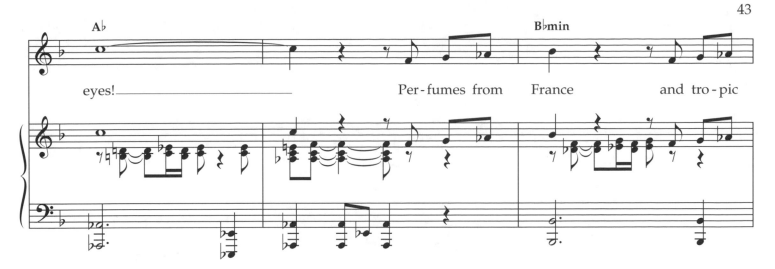

It's A Blue World

from the Columbia Motion Picture **MUSIC IN MY HEART**
(sung by Tony Martin)

Words and Music by
BOB WRIGHT and CHET FORREST

Moderately slow, steady

You were the light that bright-ened my life, My stars and moon and sun. Then with your flight came the night in my life, No laughs, no love, no fun. It's a

Moderately slow, steady

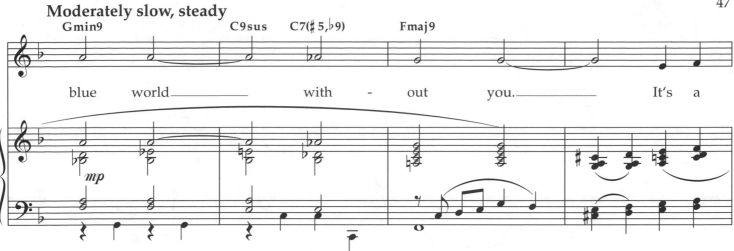

blue world _____ with - out you. _____ It's a

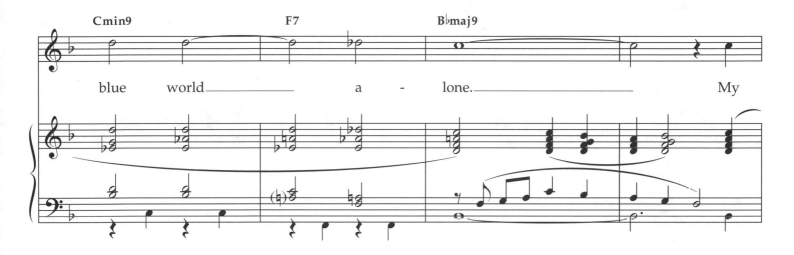

blue world _____ a - lone. _____ My

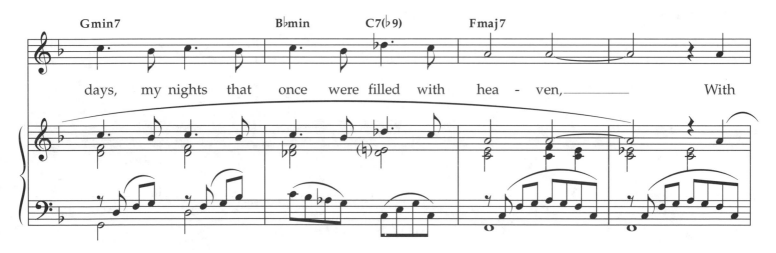

days, my nights that once were filled with hea - ven, _____ With

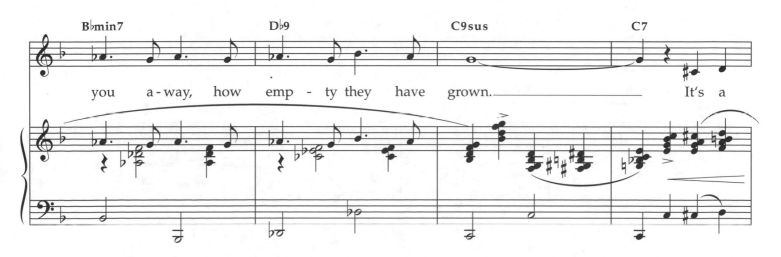

you a - way, how emp - ty they have grown. _____ It's a

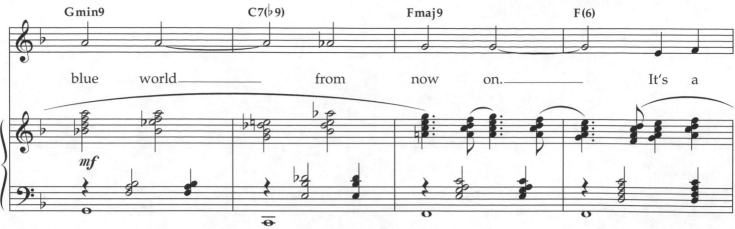

blue world_____ from now on._____ It's a

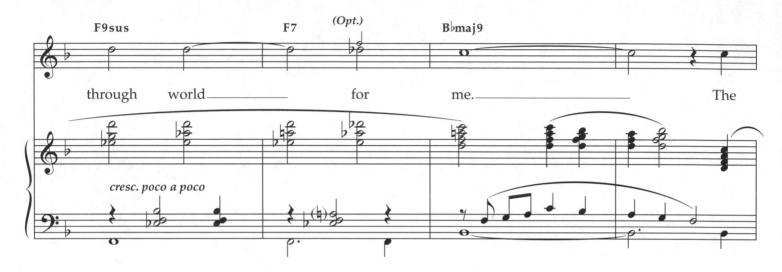

through world_____ for me._____ The

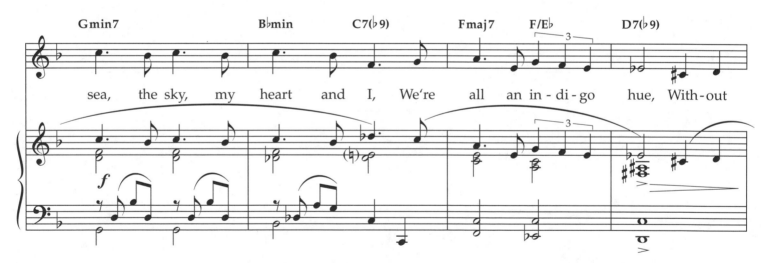

sea, the sky, my heart and I, We're all an in-di-go hue, With-out

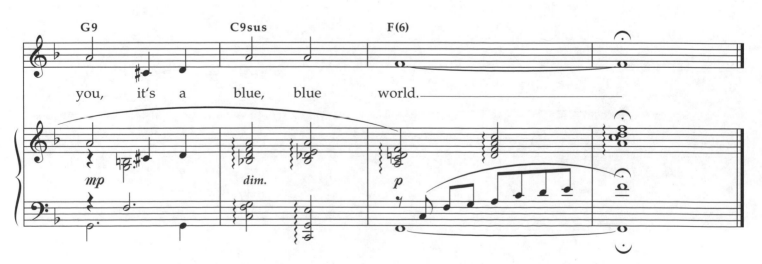

you, it's a blue, blue world._____

Little Hands

from the Broadway Musical "ANASTASIA" / "ANYA"
(sung by Lillian Gish and Constance Towers)

Music and Lyric by
ROBERT WRIGHT and GEORGE FORREST
Based on Theme of S. Rachmaninoff

Slowly, expressively and tenderly

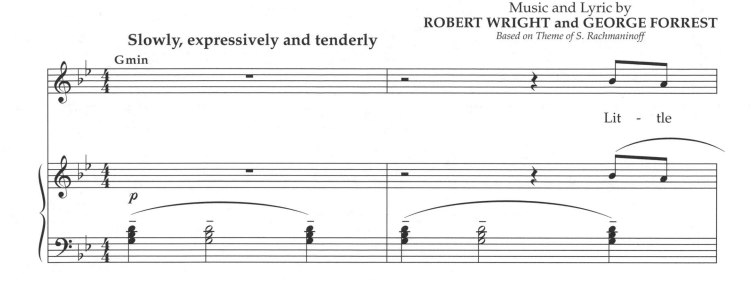

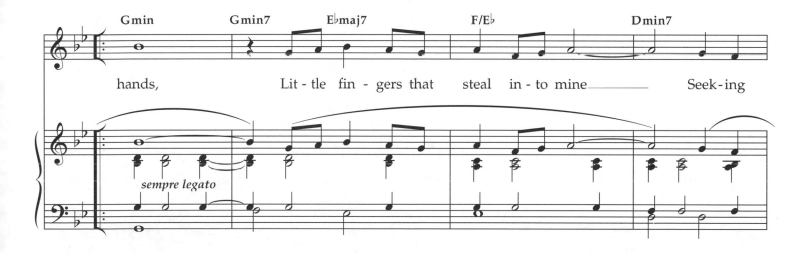

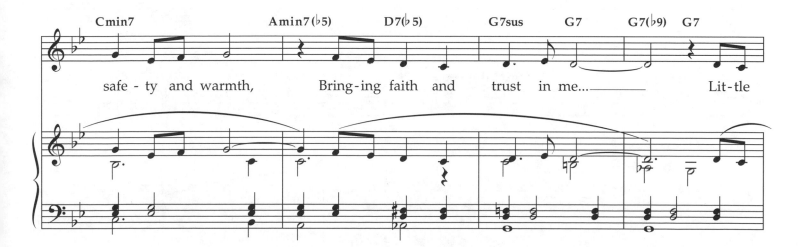

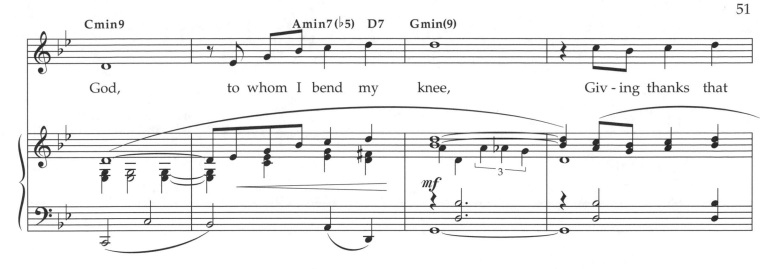

God, to whom I bend my knee, Giv-ing thanks that

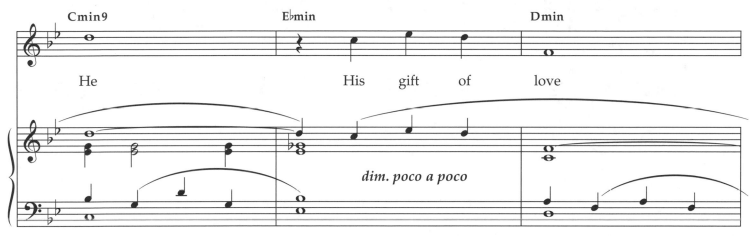

He His gift of love

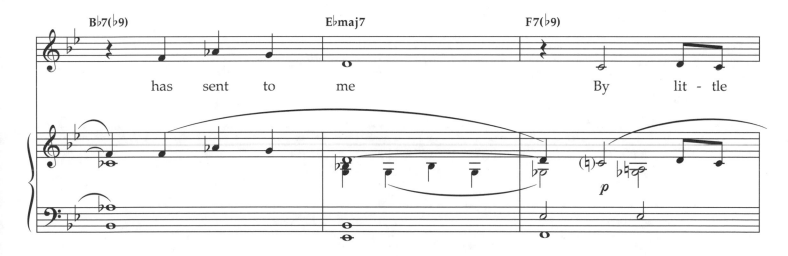

has sent to me By lit-tle

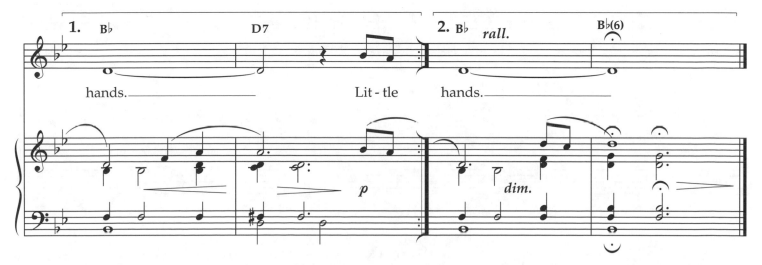

hands. Lit-tle hands.

I've Got Music In My Heart

from the Motion Picture **MUSIC IN MY HEART**

Words and Music by
BOB WRIGHT and CHET FORREST

Brightly

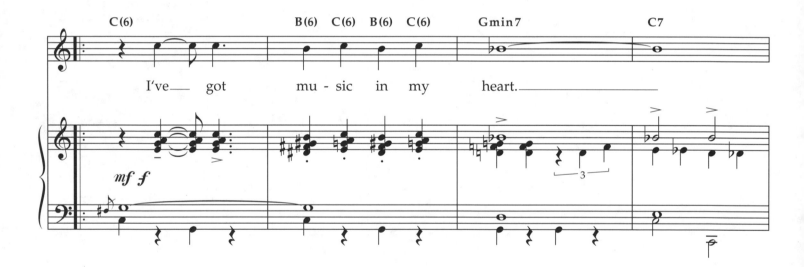

I've— got mu-sic in my heart.—

Oh!— What mu-sic in my heart.—

I can't move from this groove,— And the spell that it's wo - ven.

rhythmically

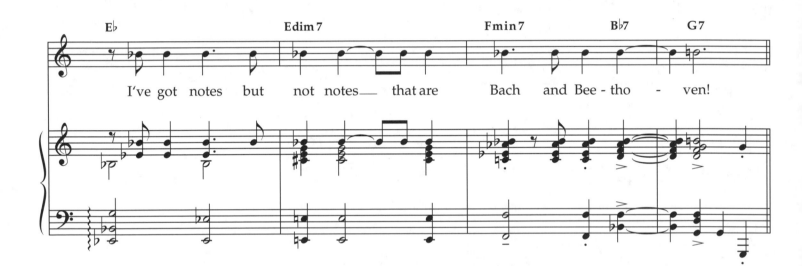

I've got notes but not notes— that are Bach and Bee - tho - ven!

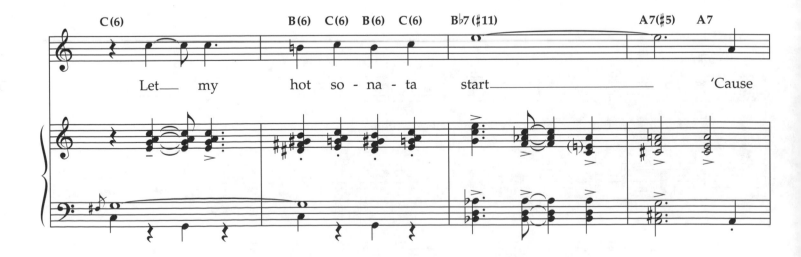

Let— my hot so - na - ta start_____ 'Cause

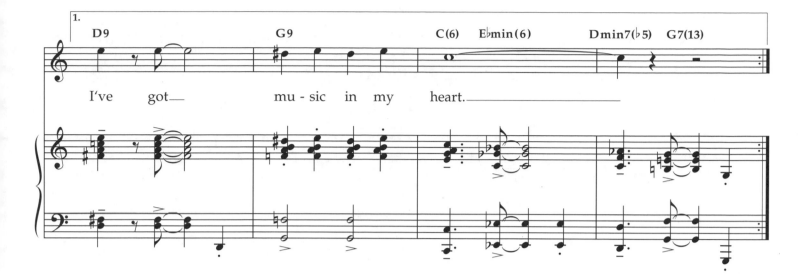

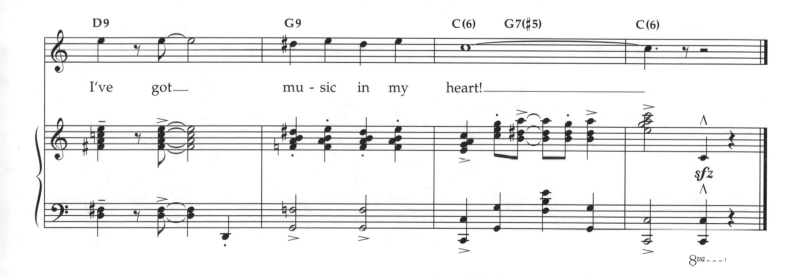

Night Of My Nights

from the MGM Motion Picture KISMET
(sung by Richard Kiley)

Words and Music by
ROBERT WRIGHT and GEORGE FORREST
Music based on themes by A. Borodin

Allegretto

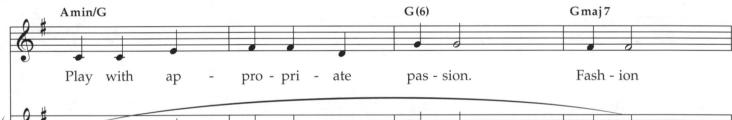

Play on the cym-bal, the tim-bal, they ly-re;

Play with ap-pro-pri-ate pas-sion. Fash-ion

songs of de-light and de-li-cious de-si-re

For the night of my nights.

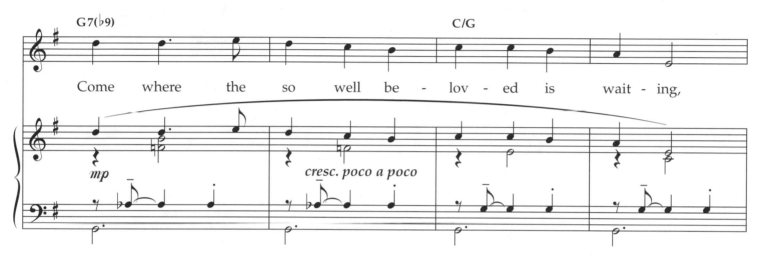

Come where the so well be - lov - ed is wait - ing,

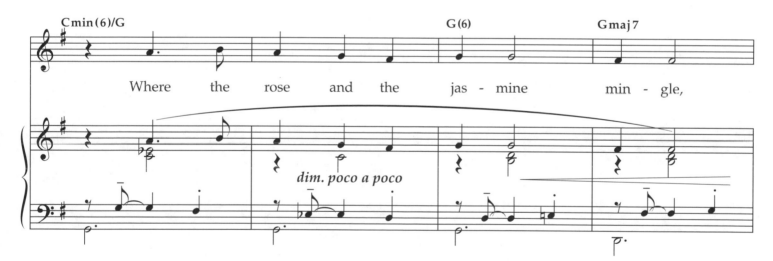

Where the rose and the jas - mine min - gle,

While I tell her the moon is for - mat - ing

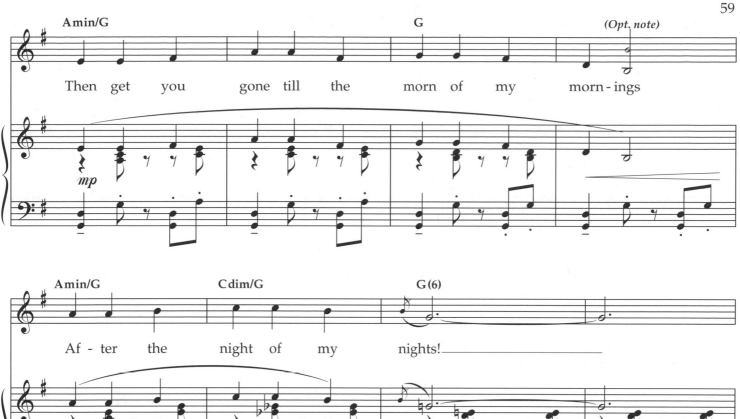

Then get you gone till the morn of my morn-ings

Af - ter the night of my nights!

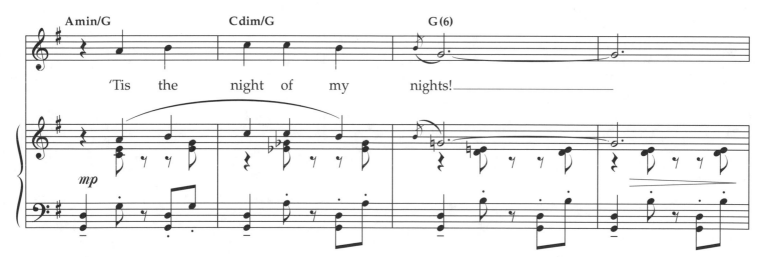

'Tis the night of my nights!

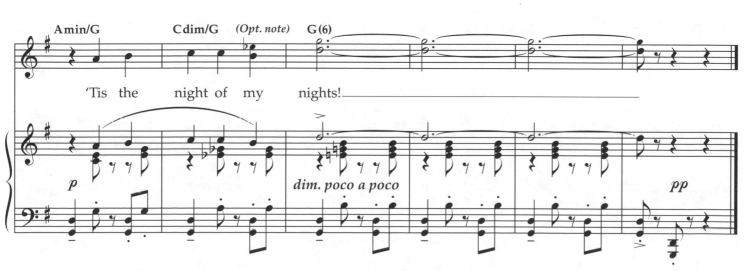

'Tis the night of my nights!

Now

from the Broadway Musical SONG OF NORWAY
(sung by Irra Petina)

Words and Music by
GEORGE CHET FORREST and ROBERT WRIGHT
based on themes of Edvard Grieg

Allegretto ma poco rubato *poco rall.*

mp delicato

a tempo

Give me to-day, Let yes-ter-day moul-der.

mp

I'll nev-er look back o-ver my shoul-der.

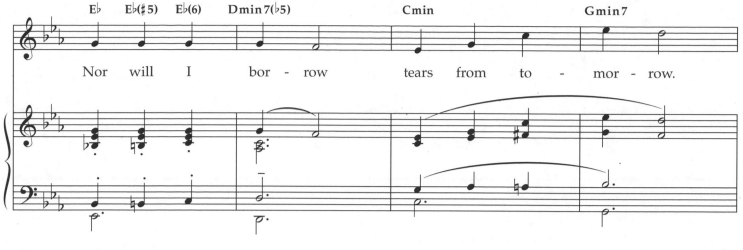

Nor will I bor - row tears from to - mor - row.

Yes - ter - day went its way, To - mor - row I'll be old - er.

Slowly, expressively

Now! Now! Not to - mor - row but now! I'll

have my heart's de - sire.

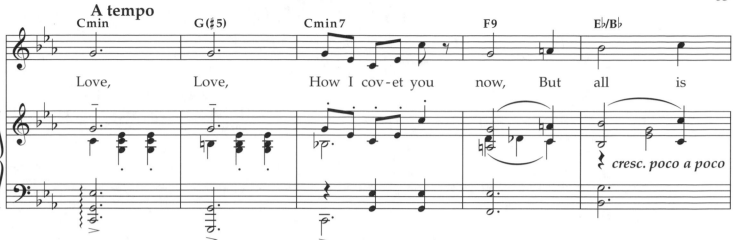

Love, Love, How I cov-et you now, But all is

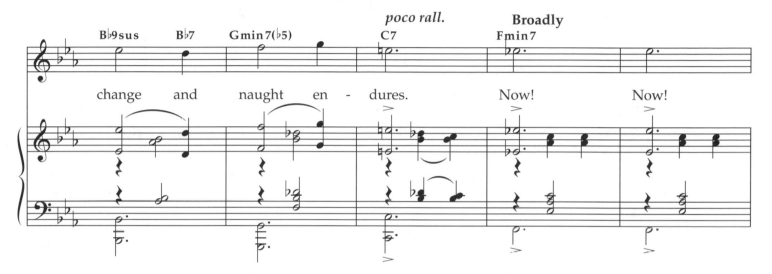

change and naught en - dures. Now! Now!

1. Not for - ev - er but Now, I'm yours!

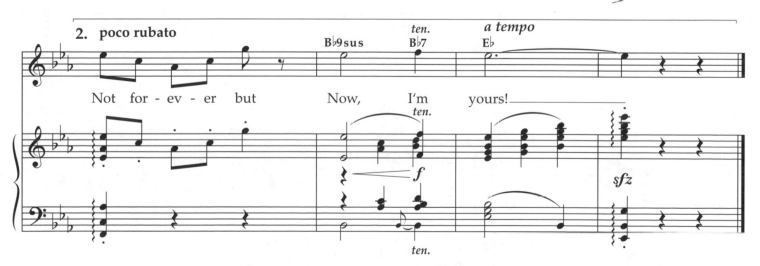

2. Not for - ev - er but Now, I'm yours!

Sands Of Time

from the MGM Motion Picture **KISMET**
(sung in the film by Howard Keel)
(sung on Broadway by Alfred Drake)

Words and Music by
ROBERT WRIGHT and GEORGE FORREST
Music based on themes of A. Borodin

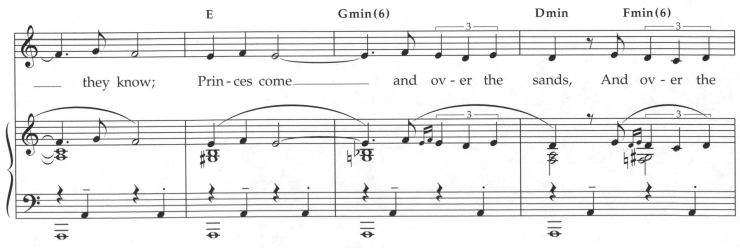

Princes come, Princes go, An hour of pomp and show they know; Princes come and over the sands, And over the

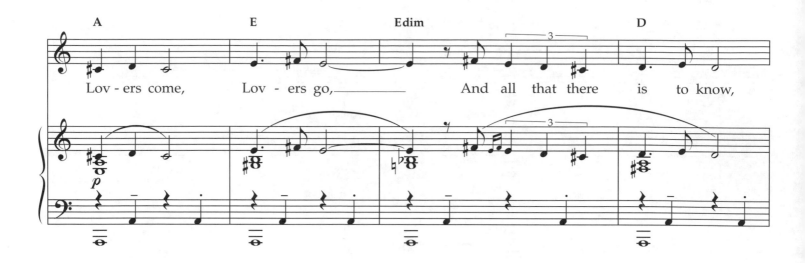

Lov - ers come, Lov - ers go,_____ And all that there is to know,

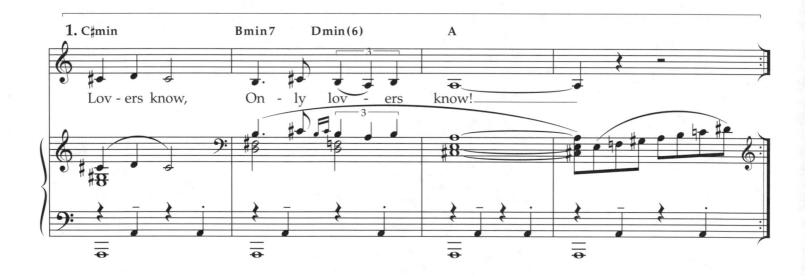

1. Lov - ers know, On - ly lov - ers know!_____

poco rall.

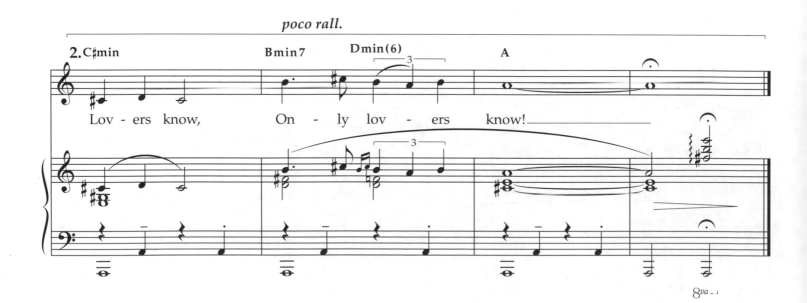

2. Lov - ers know, On - ly lov - ers know!_____

Strange Music

from the Musical **SONG OF NORWAY**
(sung on Broadway by Lawrence Brooks and Helena Bliss)
(sung in the film by Toraly Maurstad and Florence Henderson)

Musical Adaptation by
ROBERT WRIGHT and GEORGE FORREST
Based on "Nocturne" and "Wedding Day in Troldhaugen" by Edvard Grieg

Calando

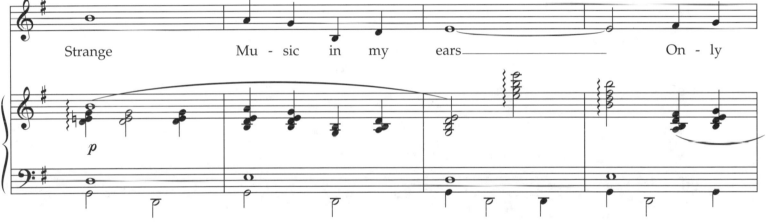

Strange Mu - sic in my ears_____ On - ly

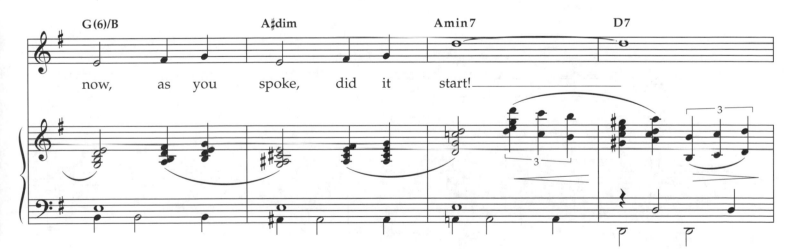

now, as you spoke, did it start!_____

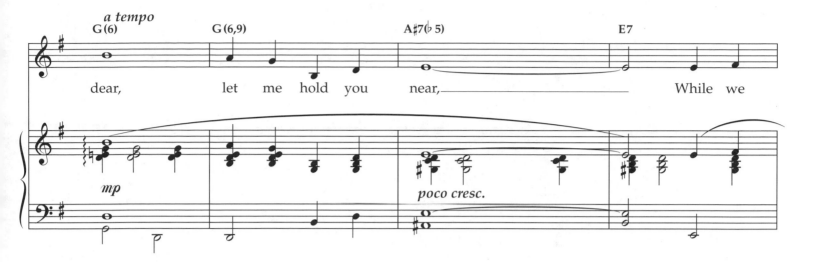

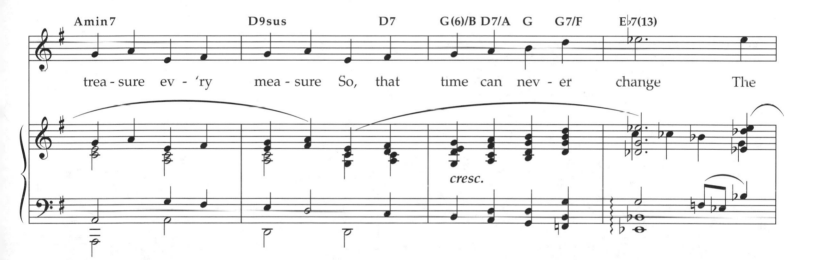

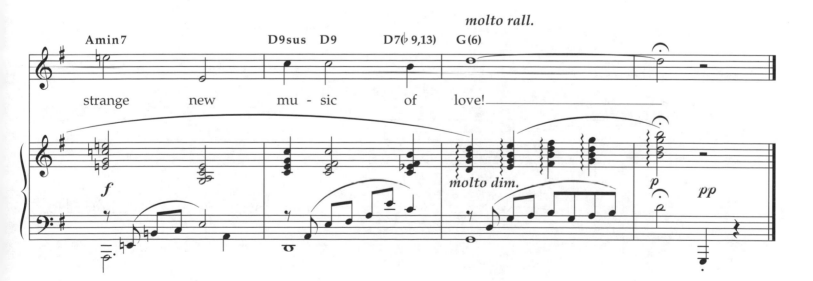

Shadows On The Sand

from the MGM Motion Picture Musical **BALALAIKA**
(sung by Nelson Eddy)

Lyrics by
BOB WRIGHT and CHET FORREST

Music adapted by
HERBERT STHOHART
Based on *SCHEHEREZADE*
by N. Rimsky-Korsakoff

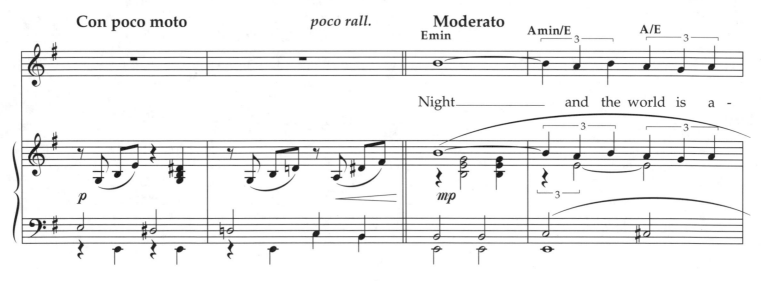

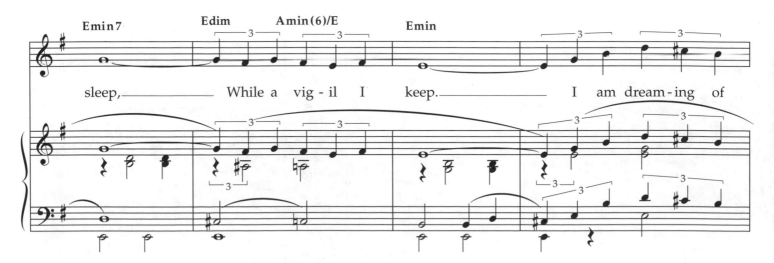

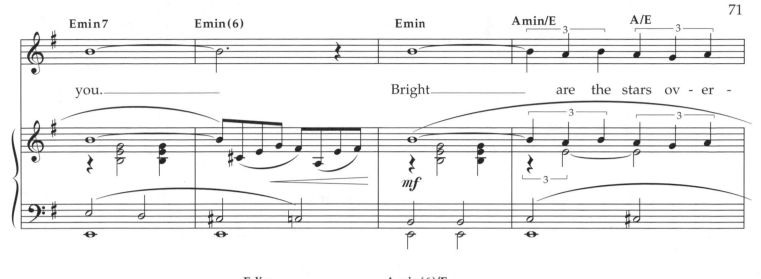

you._____ Bright_____ are the stars ov - er -

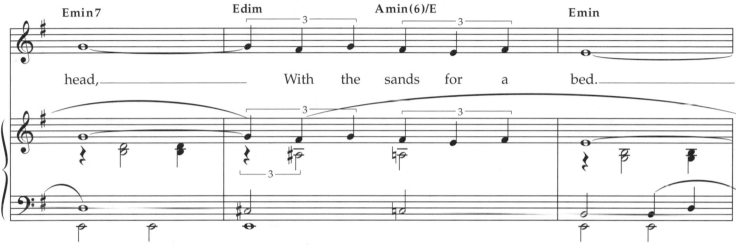

head,_____ With the sands for a bed._____

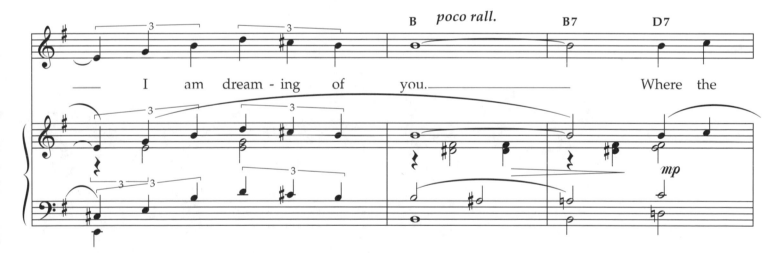

_____ I am dream - ing of you._____ Where the

Espressivo con moto

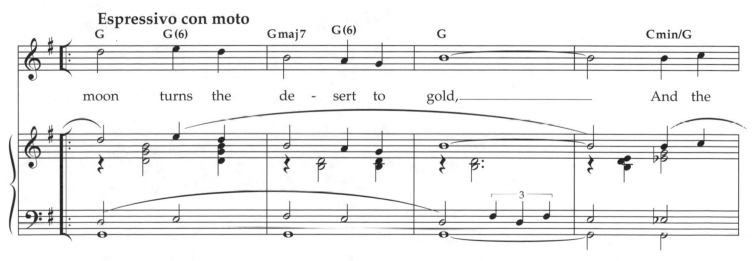

moon turns the de - sert to gold,_____ And the

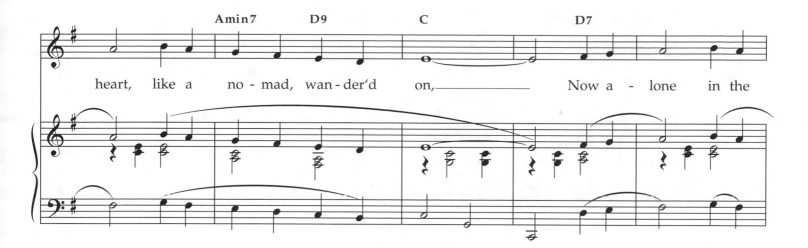

heart, like a no-mad, wan-der'd on,_____ Now a-lone in the

de-sert I stand,_____ And I dream of two sha-dows on the

sand. Where the sand._____

Stranger In Paradise

from the MGM Motion Picture Musical **KISMET**
(sung by Ann Blyth and Vic Damone)
(originally sung on Broadway by Richard Kiley)

Words and Music by
ROBERT WRIGHT and GEORGE FORREST
Music based on themes of A. Borodin

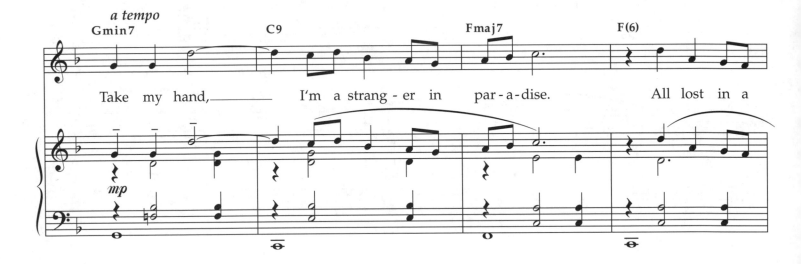

Take my hand,_____ I'm a strang-er in par-a-dise.
All lost in a

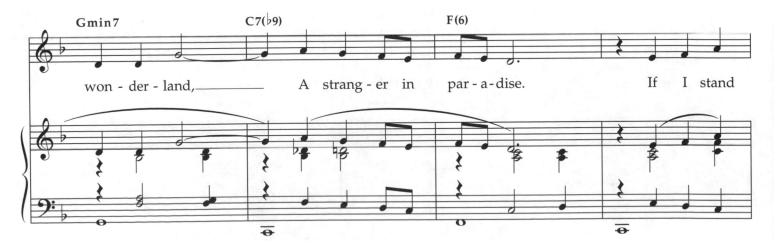

won-der-land,_____ A strang-er in par-a-dise. If I stand

star - ry eyed,_____ That's a dan - ger in par-a dise For mor - tals who

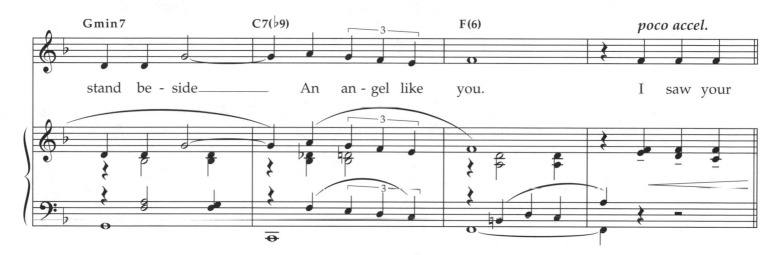

stand be - side_____ An an - gel like you. I saw your

Con moto

face_____ And I as - cend - ed_____ Out of the

com - mon-place_____ In - to the rare! Some-where in

dark des - pair____ From all that I hun-ger for, But o - pen your

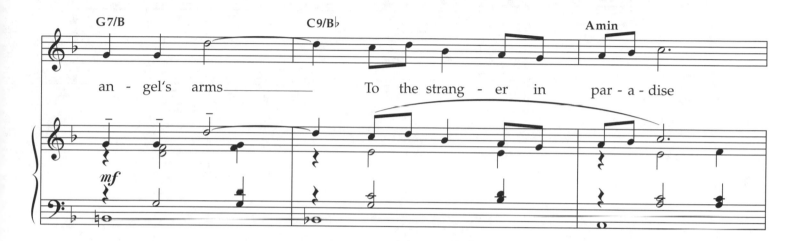

an - gel's arms____ To the strang - er in par - a - dise

And tell him that he need be____ A strang - er no

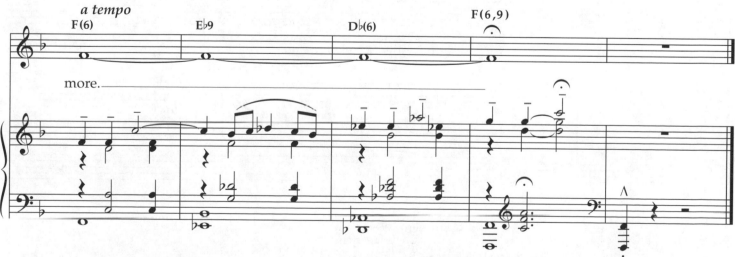

more.____

Three Loves

*from the Broadway Musical **SONG OF NORWAY***
(sung by Irra Petina)

Words and Music by
GEORGE CHET FORREST and ROBERT WRIGHT
Based on themes of Edvard Grieg

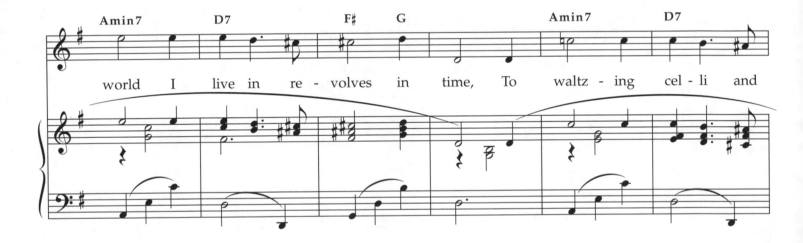

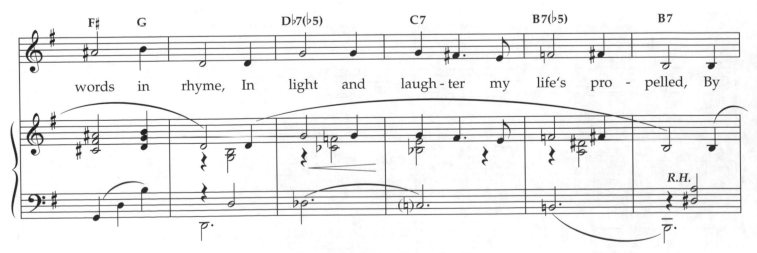

whose two arms I am held in.

Three loves have I,_____ Three a - flame in my

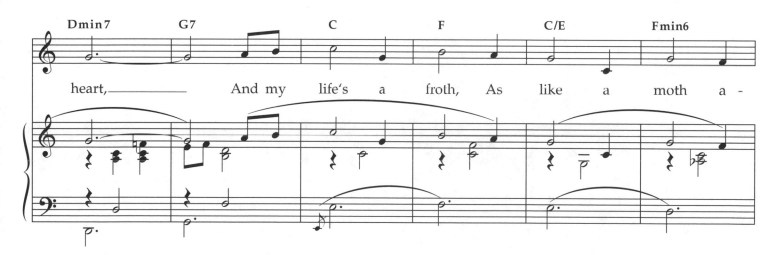

heart,_____ And my life's a froth, As like a moth a -

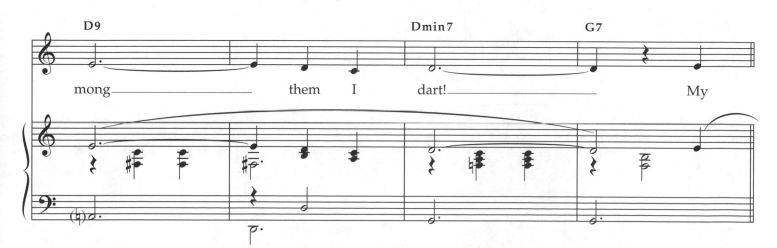

mong_____ them I dart!_____ My

first love is to laugh,_____ An - oth - er love is to

sing,_____ My third and great - est is my love of

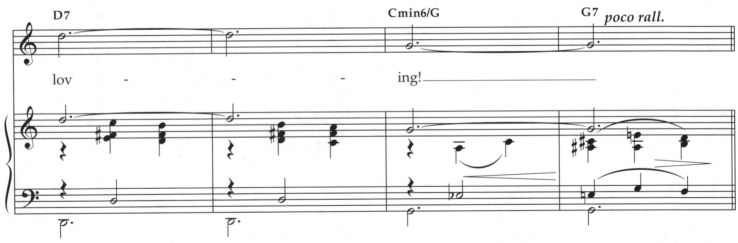

lov - - - ing!_____

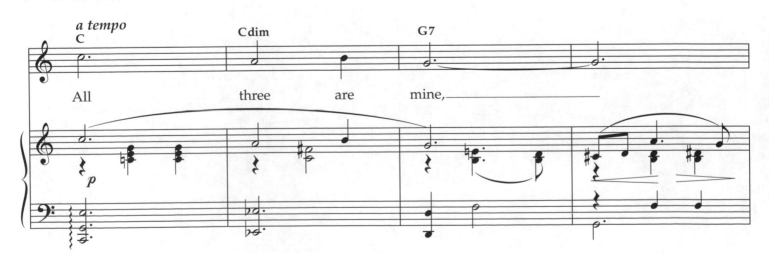

All three are mine,_____

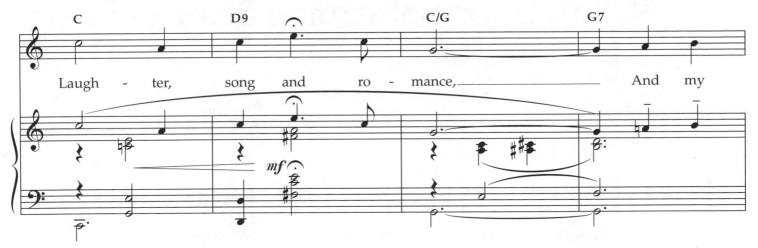

Laugh - ter, song and ro - mance,_____ And my

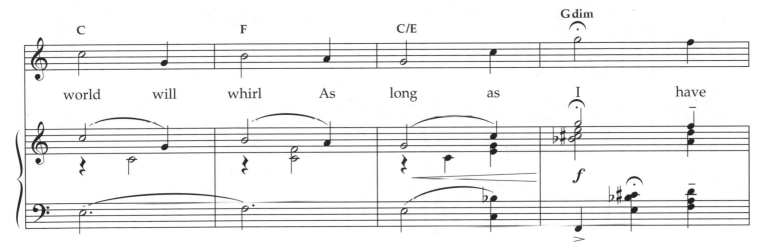

world will whirl As long as I have

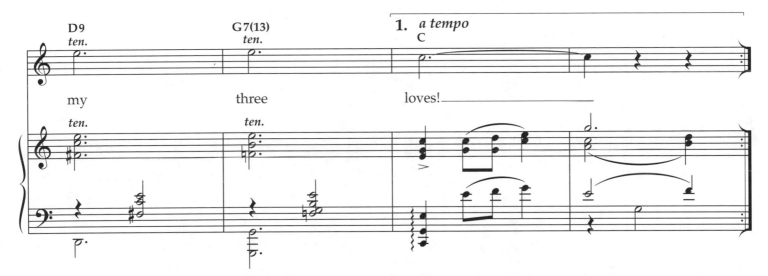

my three loves!_____

loves!_____

Think Upon Something Beautiful

*from the Musical **ANASTASIA / ANYA***
(sung by Constance Towers, Lillian Gish, Judy Kaye and Regina Resnick)

Music and Lyric by
ROBERT WRIGHT and GEORGE FORREST

Slowly, expressively

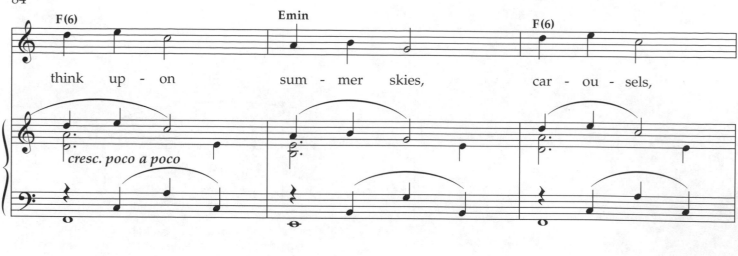

think up - on sum - mer skies, car - ou - sels,

cresc. poco a poco

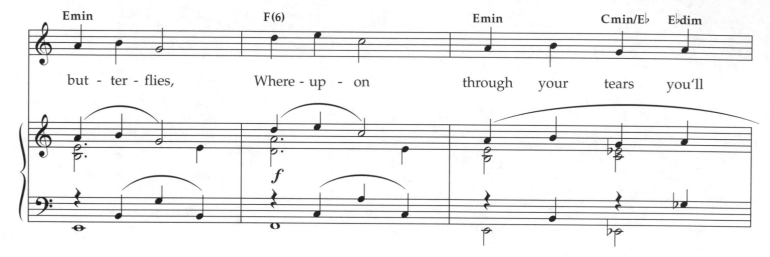

but - ter - flies, Where - up - on through your tears you'll

f

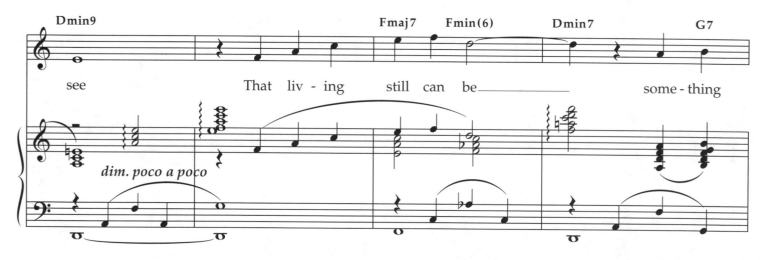

see That liv - ing still can be_____ some - thing

dim. poco a poco

beau - ti - ful,___ beau - ti - ful,___ beau - ti - ful.___

p   *pp*

To Look Upon My Love

from the Broadway Musical Comedy KEAN
(sung by Alfred Drake)

Music and Lyric by
ROBERT WRIGHT and GEORGE FORREST

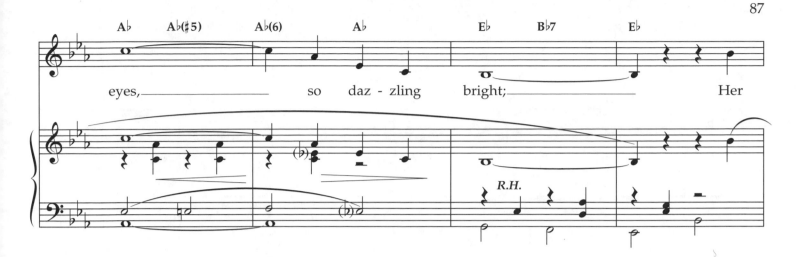

eyes,_____ so daz - zling bright;_____ Her

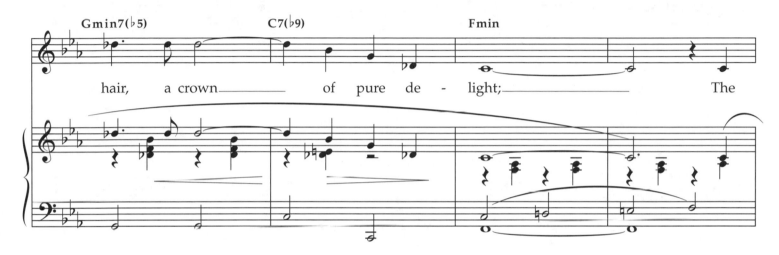

hair, a crown_____ of pure de - light;_____ The

wit and warmth_____ her smiles re - veal_____ Un -

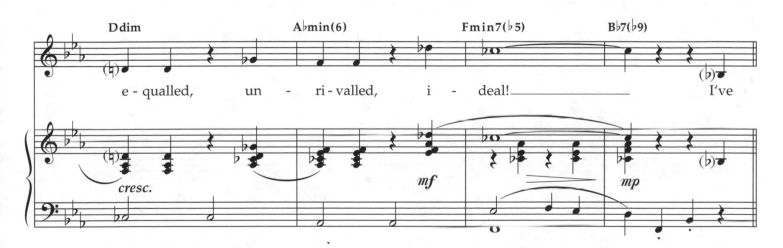

e - qualled, un - ri - valled, i - deal!_____ I've

seen the ris - ing sun, I've viewed the cres - cent moon, I've

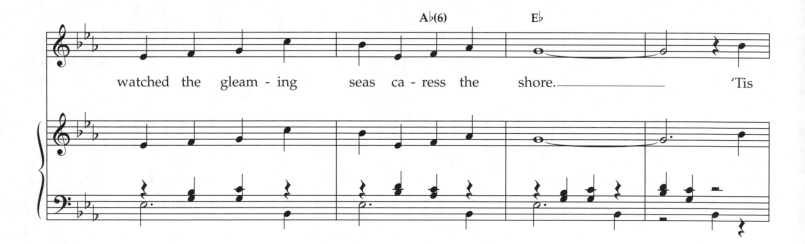

watched the gleam - ing seas ca - ress the shore.———————— 'Tis

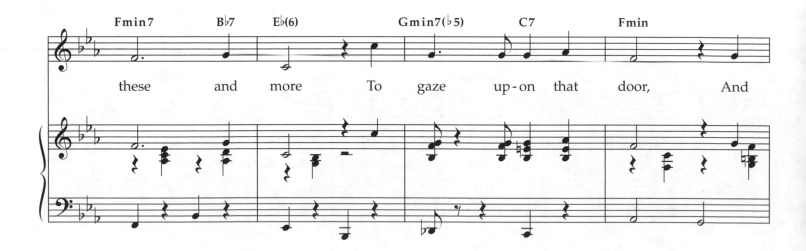

these and more To gaze up-on that door, And

know that an-y mo - ment it will give_____ And I'll

look up-on my love_____ and

cresc. poco a poco

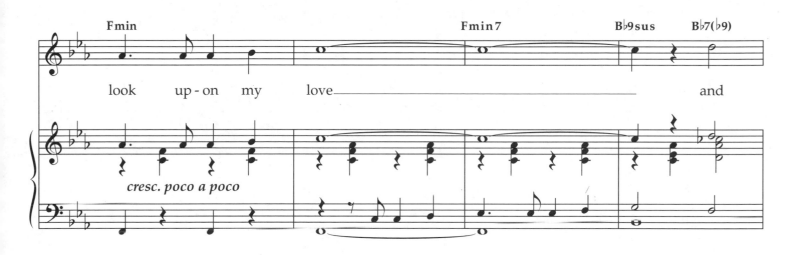

1. Eb

live!_____ Rare

f *dim. poco a poco* *mp*

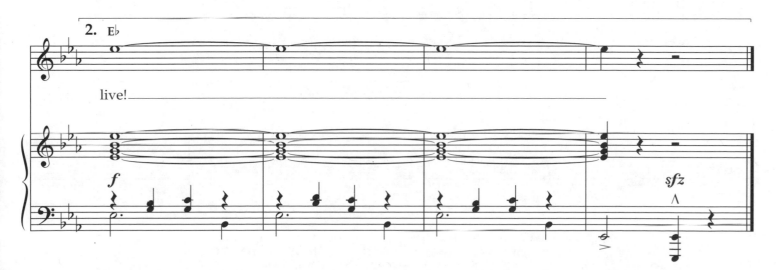

2. Eb

live!_____

f *sfz*

We'll Take A Glass Together

from the Musical **GRAND HOTEL**

Music and Lyrics by
ROBERT WRIGHT and GEORGE FORREST

Rhythmic and not too fast

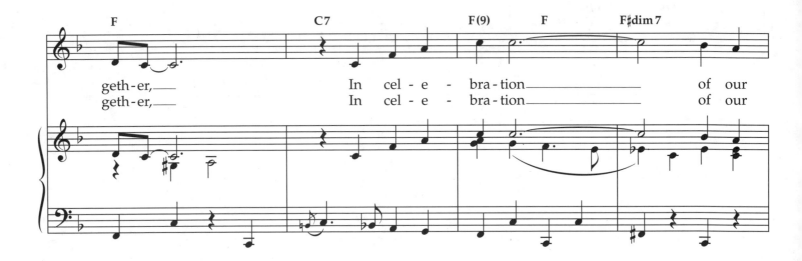

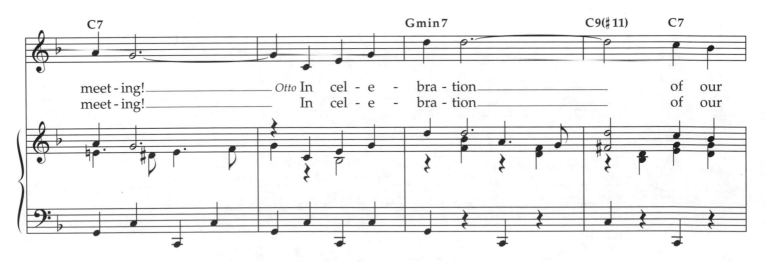

92

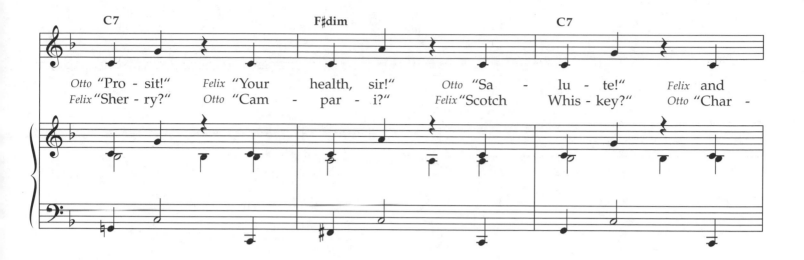

Otto "Pro - sit!" Felix "Your health, sir!" Otto "Sa - lu - te!" Felix and
Felix "Sher - ry?" Otto "Cam - par - i?" Felix "Scotch Whis - key?" Otto "Char -

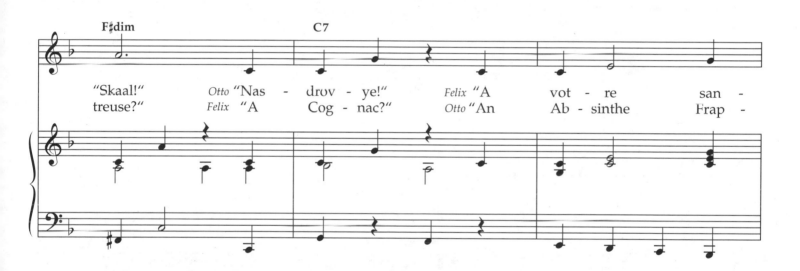

"Skaal!" Otto "Nas - drov - ye!" Felix "A vot - re san -
treuse?" Felix "A Cog - nac?" Otto "An Ab - sinthe Frap -

te!" Felix For one warm mo - ment In a
pe!" Otto For one warm mo - ment In a

What You Need

*from the Musical **GRAND HOTEL***

Music and Lyrics by
ROBERT WRIGHT and GEORGE FORREST

Moderately

What you need_____ Is some-one strong_____ To

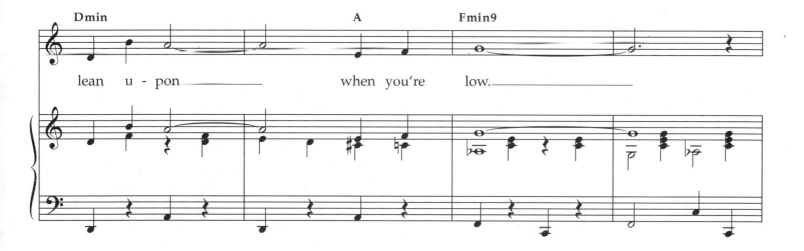

lean u - pon_____ when you're low._____

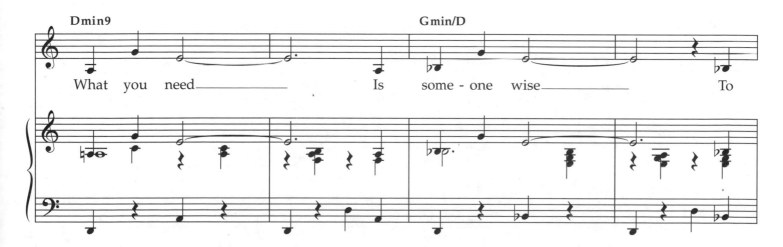

What you need_____ Is some-one wise_____ To

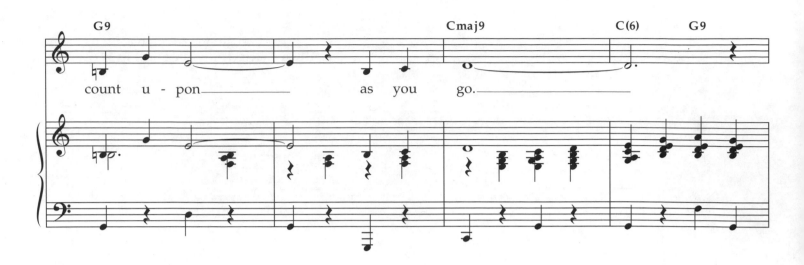

count u - pon____ as you go.____

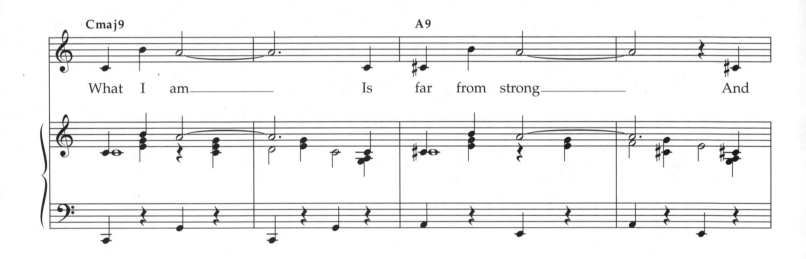

What I am____ Is far from strong____ And

far from wise,____ Oh, far in - deed!____ Yet

sud - den - ly,_____ When you cling to me,_____ I feel

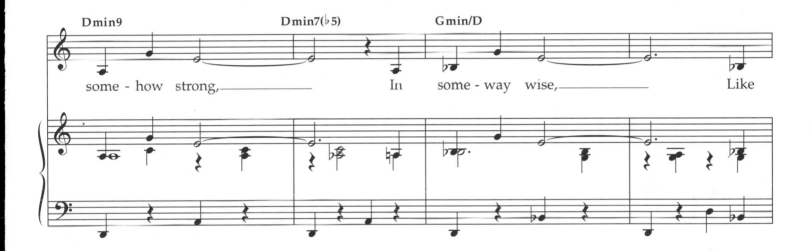

some - how strong,_____ In some - way wise,_____ Like

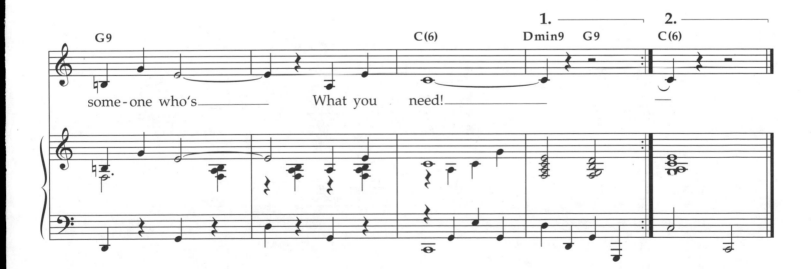

some - one who's_____ What you need!_____

Willow, Willow, Willow

from the Broadway Musical Comedy KEAN
(sung by Lee Venora)

Music and Lyrics by
ROBERT WRIGHT and GEORGE FORREST

Slowly and simply

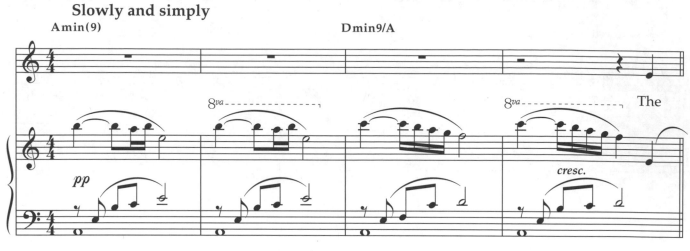

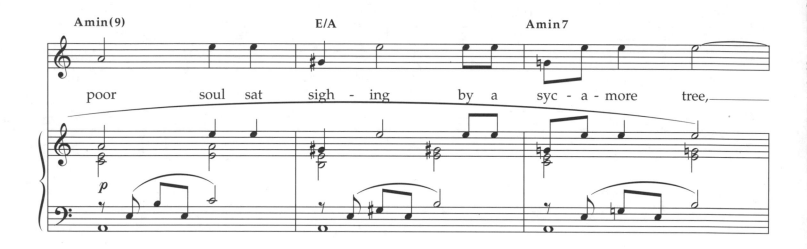

poor soul sat sigh - ing by a syc - a - more tree,

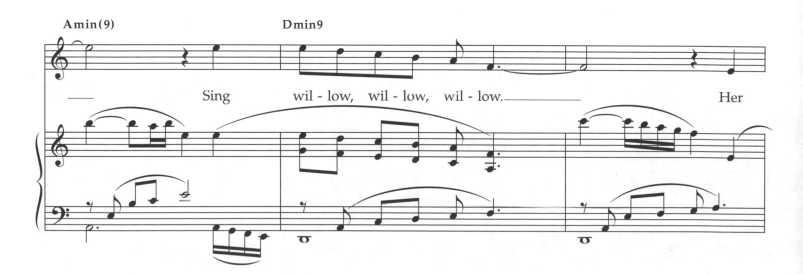

Sing wil - low, wil - low, wil - low. Her

Con poco moto

salt tears fell from her and soft - en'd the stones; Sing

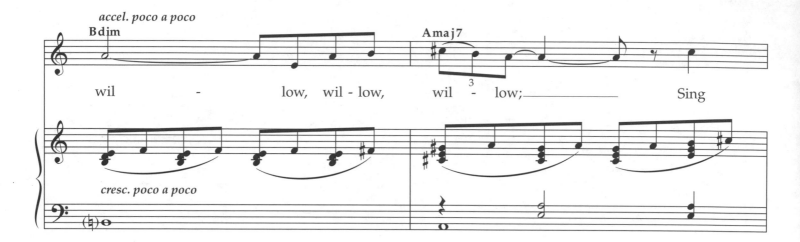

wil - low, wil - low, wil - low; Sing

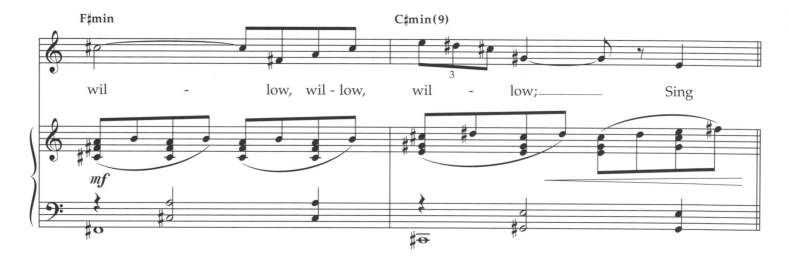

wil - low, wil - low, wil - low; Sing

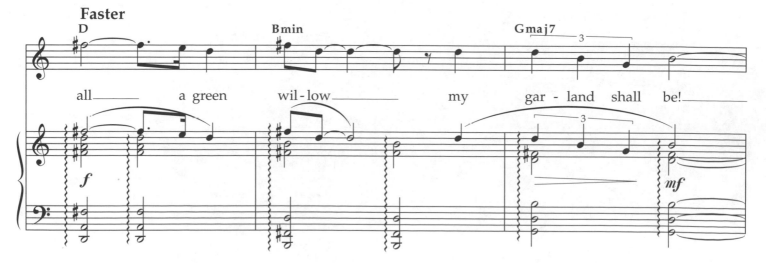

all a green wil - low my gar - land shall be!

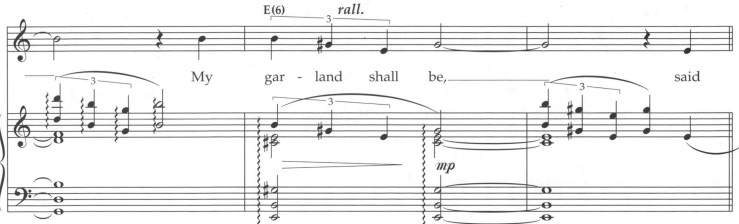

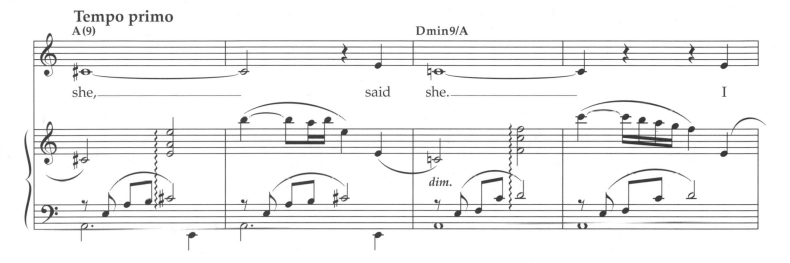

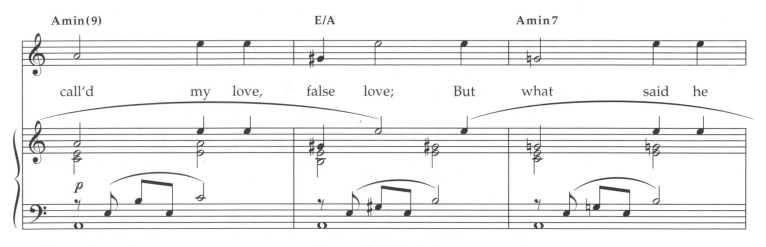

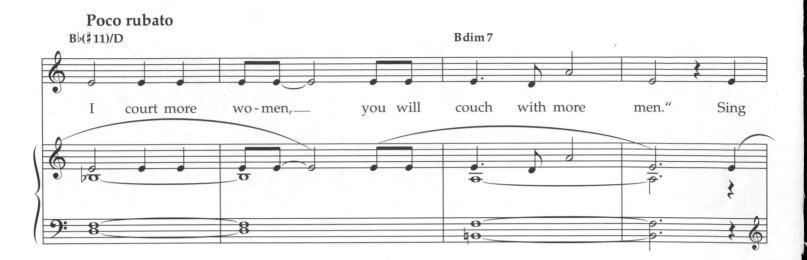

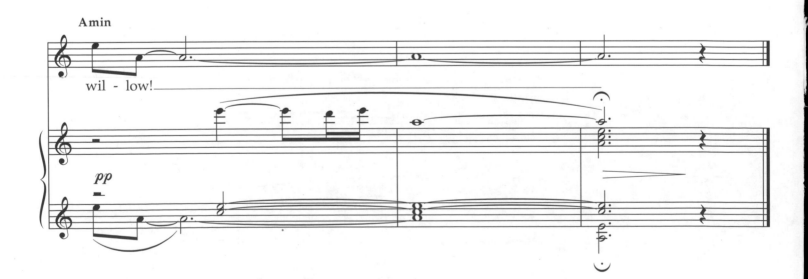